I0533379

HOODOO

M.C. PEAK

HANGAR 1 PUBLISHING

Copyright © 2025 by M.C. Peak

All rights reserved.

No part of this book may be reproduced in any form or by any electronic or mechanical means, including information storage and retrieval systems, without written permission from the author, except for the use of brief quotations in a book review.

PROLOGUE

No one knows for sure when or how it all began. Some say it was conjured into existence by the old ones, the original guardians of the land, to punish those who would disrespect it. Those who would cheapen life in search of riches in fur and gold.

Whether or not one believes in the stories is irrelevant. The fact is that something is there and has been there since before recorded history, watching, waiting. Waiting for the next wayward soul to blaspheme the land. To disrespect the unwritten laws of nature. The stories of this legendary creature can be verified if one is only willing to look. The stories are well documented and are not pleasant. They are tales one might tell around a campfire, hoping to raise the hairs on the necks of those unfamiliar with the legend and reignite fear in the hearts of those who are.

Most folks who live in the hills and lands around the mountain don't speak of the legend lightly. There have been too many coincidences, too many signs to ignore, and, more importantly, too many people gone missing never to be seen again. Most people tread lightly when up on the mountain. Its very name comes from Native Americans, who called the mountain Hoodoo, which loosely translates to mountain devil. It is also the name they gave to the creature who lived there. Or would it be more accurate to say, *lives* there?

Native American tribes all over speak of large, hairy, bipedal creatures. Most believe they represent a link between man and nature, acting as protectors of the natural order. Many Native tribes call them the lost tribe — a tribe of creatures that chooses to be lost. Not lost in the sense most would think of, but lost as in not wanting to be found. Some tribes call it a thief, a cannibal, an evil trickster. The Hoodoo fall into this description.

The first recorded story of the Hoodoo was in October 1879, by a prospector named Silas Brogan. Brogan came to Hoodoo Mountain in search of the gold rumored to be there. Gold was found in Hoodoo Creek, but the mother lode was said to be in a vein somewhere near the summit.

Brogan spent months digging along a drainage that fed into Hoodoo Creek, finding small deposits of the allusive gold rock but nothing large. Brogan journaled that he felt as if he was being watched and the woods around him were deathly quiet. He attributed this to the possibility he was being watched by the Kalispel, or the Salish, also known as Flatheads. Maybe even the Kootenai Tribe. These were all Native tribes that hunted and lived in this area. Although he never saw any sign of humans anywhere.

One October morning, Brogan was awakened by a blood-curdling scream that seemed to come from the very bowels of the mountain itself., shaking the tall timbers that surrounded his camp. In his journal, Brogan noted a "foul smelling stench that turned his stomach. The smell was almost as putrid flesh." Brogan spent that night wide awake and clutching his prized Springfield Trapdoor Carbine chambered in .50 caliber. The Trapdoor used rimfire technology instead of the traditional musket-style rifle of the day. This allowed for faster firing and easier reloading, a must in the untamed wilderness of the great Northwest. But it would be to no avail, as Brogan would soon find out.

Brogan writes of finding his mining equipment destroyed and "large, almost human-like footprints amongst the damage." He measured the footprints at over nineteen inches with what appeared to be toes that seemed more clawlike than toelike. One of Brogan's shovels was snapped in two, and a sluice box, used to separate gold from the sand and gravel, was crushed beyond repair. But most notable in his entry on this day was a description of what most have called the Hoodoo.

From Brogan's journal dated October 29, 1879: "While collecting my tools and property that had been scattered throughout the drainage, I noticed that foul stench from last night. I turned to retrieve my Springfield and saw a glimpse of a creature some yards away and glaring at me as if passing unfavorable judgement upon my soul. I felt paralyzed with fear but the creature made no attempt to approach me. The creature abruptly issued a short, breathy, scream and ran deeper into the woods away from me. I marked the location where I last saw it and slowly made my way there. I estimate the creature was between eight and nine feet tall, covered in long, shaggy, white hair with a muscular build. There were tracks at the location that matched those from the drainage. I am being watched."

This would be the last entry in Brogan's journal. Accounts by those who came upon the devastation said no body was ever found, just evidence of a violent struggle. Brogan's rifle was found smashed and broken. There were empty shell casings scattered around the camp as if he were shooting at shadows. The camp was destroyed and, according to those who happened upon the scene, there were numerous large footprints throughout the area that seemed to be everywhere yet led nowhere. They all reported one other thing as well. A foul, lingering stench permeated the site. The Kalispel elders in the area said Brogan must have angered the Hoodoo by desecrating the land and was punished by it. That theory was mocked as silly Native superstition. Most people attributed the incident to claim jumpers, outlaws, or renegade Indians.

The years from Brogan's demise up on Hoodoo Mountain until modern day would be filled with strange stories of sightings of a monstrous, white-haired beast that roamed the mountain and surrounding areas. Unexplained disappearances, suicides, hauntings, strange lights, and eerie sounds fill the folklore of settlers and Natives alike.

It has been called the Old Man of the Woods, the Hoodoo Howler, the Hairy Ghost, and Bigfoot. The Kalispel would eventually call the creature or creatures that lived on the mountain Seatco, or stick Indian. The Indian that lived in the woods. Whatever the moniker, one thing is certain: as far as the Brogan incident, the Kalispel were right.

1

TUESDAY, JULY 4, 2015

"C'mon, Brandon! Geez, you're as slow as a fucking snail." Steve Rucker and his brother, Brandon, were hustling up the side of Hoodoo Mountain with a box of fireworks. They were planning on setting them off from the top of the mountain for a Fourth of July show no one had ever done before. They were making good time getting up the mountain, the advantage of being early twenty-somethings. But youth was not an excuse for the remarkably idiotic plan they had hatched. Setting off mortar fireworks during the height of the fire season was illegal, not to mention just plain stupid. And this was a particularly dry year.

"Are you sure this is a good idea, Steve? It's awfully dry up here."

Steve laughed off his brother's concern. "Damn! Quit being such a baby. It's mostly rocks up there."

Steve's tone let Brandon know to shut up and put up. He changed the subject. "Hey, Steve. You believe all the stories about this mountain?"

Steve stopped, kicking up a cloud of dust, and looked Brandon right in the eyes. "Are you fucking shittin' me? Don't tell me you're scared the Hoodoo's gonna get you. It's just a bunch of stupid made-up stories. I've hunted these hills for years, and I've never seen anything strange in these woods. You're killin' me."

Brandon didn't answer. He didn't want his brother thinking he was a wimp or something, but he couldn't shake the feeling they were being watched. And there was that whiff of something... He couldn't quite place it. It was faint but foul.

"Of course not, bro. But there are a lot of folks, dad included, that say there's something up here. Something not normal." He tried to sound nonchalant, but there was a hint of fear in his voice. "Do you remember the story dad told us about his elk being taken one night? There were strange footprints and no evidence of the elk being dragged. Five hundred pounds of elk meat just carried out of camp never to be seen again. Just sayin' it's kinda weird, that's all."

"Jesus, Brandon. Dad just told us that story to scare us. He would tell the story every damn time we came up here just to see our reaction."

"You're probably right. Where do you want to light these bad boys off?"

"Now you're talkin'. Just up there on that rock outcrop. It looks over all of Blanchard below. Shit! People will be talkin' about the fireworks show on Hoodoo Mountain for years. We'll be legends."

The two brothers reached the rock outcrop just before dark. They set up their fireworks array and waited for the perfect time to light them off.

"All right, Brandon. I got all the mortars connected with the dynamite fuse. One light of the fuse, and all the damn mortars will go off in succession. It will be a thing of beauty."

Brandon got himself in position to light the fuse. "Geez! What the fuck is that smell?"

Steve shrugged. "Probably just a skunk. Let 'er rip!"

Brandon lit the fuse, and the two brothers jumped back to watch the show.

Boom! The first mortar blasted skyward and exploded in a wondrous shower of white sparks. *Boom!* Another mortar. Then another, until all their pyrotechnics were spent. It was a beautiful sight, but one of their mortars hit the tinder-dry forest, and the undergrowth started to burn.

"Oh, *shit!*" Steve's voice was panicky. "I think we just started a fucking forest fire. Let's get the hell outta here." They'd be legends, all right. Legendary fire starters.

"What the fuck is that damn smell?" Brandon turned to look back over his shoulder. "Oh, fuck, no! Steve! What the hell is *that*?"

No one heard their screams. No one felt their fear. No one saw their fate. At least they weren't alone when the mountain swallowed them up.

They were blamed for the fire on Hoodoo Mountain, and everyone figured they'd skipped town. The mountain gained another mystery, and the county gained a nasty fire.

2

FIRE SITREP BRIEFING, JULY 5, 2015

"Let's get it together, ladies and gentlemen." Captain John "JC" Robertson was starting the briefing on the current status and plan of attack for several forest fires in the North Idaho Panhandle region. A seasoned veteran of fifteen years of fighting fires in every corner of North Idaho, Robertson had been in just about every situation a firefighter could be in and survive. This fire would be like none other he had experienced. He had the weathered brow of a man who had spent most of his life in nature's crucible of fire and heat, and he wore it well. Even though this year would mark his fiftieth on earth, he had the physique and stamina of men half his age, a benefit of hauling heavy gear up and down steep and rugged terrain.

"We've got a busy stretch ahead of us. First, let me say this — Mother Nature is going to be a real mother over the next ten days. No rain in sight, high winds, and it's gonna be hotter than hell. Hydrate, hydrate, hydrate. This has been an extremely active fire season so far, so we are gonna be stretched *thin*."

A drier than normal winter and spring, capped by a succession of windy days, kicked off this year's fire season. Dry lightning started most of the fires, a phenomenon caused by thunderstorms whose rainfall evaporates before hitting the ground. But human negligence or ignorance of the fire risks caused several of the fires.

Captain Robertson looked out over his crew of about twenty fire-fighters. They were tired, dirty, and disheveled from weeks on the fire lines, but they still had plenty of fight in them. His was a dedicated mix of professionals and volunteers.

Ben Proctor was a mountain of a man, with ten years in the fire service. He stood six feet four inches and was strong as an ox. Ben would head up Team A.

Sam Reynolds was a contrast in extremes to Ben — portly and only a hair over five feet tall, but what he lacked in size, he made up for in spirit and sense of humor. Everyone called him Stumpy due to his short, stocky, build. As B team leader, he once stayed awake for three days cutting a fire break over some of the most rugged terrain in North Idaho. That effort saved a lot of lives and property.

Nancy Mills would lead C team. She didn't look like the type to suit up and fight forest fires. She looked more like she should be a model in some fashion magazine. With dazzling green eyes and short auburn hair, she seemed more suited to a corporate career than to the smelly, dirty, and dangerous one she preferred. Slim, trim, and athletically built, she was the perfect fit to lead Team C, which mostly comprised of experienced volunteers originally chosen from a pool of college students from the surrounding area. Team C was fast and had boundless energy, as one would expect from a group of eighteen- to twenty-somethings. Nancy had spent her whole life in Northern Idaho and obtained her forestry degree from the University of Idaho just five years ago. She hand picked this group two years ago when named team leader. Her crew knew what to do and were usually tasked with flanking moves to surround the fire so it could be contained, controlled, and eventually snuffed out.

"Settle down! Bring it in, people! Today's gonna be fun." Fun. That usually meant a trip to hell and hopefully back. "We got us a suspected arson in Blanchard up near the Hoodoo. There's a lot of homes scattered up in those hills, so we need to move fast." Nancy knew what that meant: C team would head in first. "C team! Mills, get

9

your crew in there and see how much ground you can cover by tomorrow. It's pretty rough country in there, so be as careful as you can. I don't want any of your kids getting hurt in there. Rescues take too much effort."

"Ha, ha, Captain. You crack me up." There might have been just a touch of sarcasm in Nancy's response.

"I want your team to get above the fire and clear the fuel just below the ridge. It's pretty rugged up there, so be careful. Once you have enough cleared, you'll start a back-burn, and hopefully we can get that going before those high winds the weather reports are calling for."

Forest fires create their own winds. As the fire consumes more and more fuel, it needs oxygen to grow. The fire will actually suck air from in front of it, creating a wind that will move any fire in front of it towards the main fire. Once the fuel is consumed, the main fire can be starved out. It is a very effective way to get control of a fire.

Ben looked over at Stumpy and said, "All right, Stumpy, don't slow us down!"

"Don't worry about me, Sasquatch." Stumpy could hold his own with Ben's ribbing. It was all in good fun, and they even had their respective "handles" written on their hard hats.

"Don't forget who saved whose ass up on Scotchman Peak. I don't want you doing anything stupid where I have to come in and save your ass again."

Stumpy was referring to Ben's ill-fated attempt to outrun a fire line that changed directions when the wind shifted. Ben had led his team into a boxed-in cliff with the fire closing in on his team. Stumpy had happened to have his crew above the fire and close to the cliff where they were trapped. Stumpy's team had secured lines above Ben and his team, and they were able to climb out of danger. Stumpy brought that up every chance he got. It was a salt-in-the-wound kind of thing, but it didn't bother Ben much. The two shared a sacred camaraderie only those who have been so close to death understand.

"Geez, you two." Nancy rolled her eyes at the banter. "Why don't you guys just kiss and get it over with already?" She tried not to show her desire to be the one kissing Ben. No pun intended, but she'd had the hots for Ben since the first time they met. Who could blame her? He was a good-looking tall drink of water.

Truth be told, Ben was more than attracted to Nancy as well. Neither had ever said a thing to the other on this subject, but there was an unspoken thing between them. Some might call it sexual tension. Everyone saw it, but no one talked about it. Well, at least not in front of them. That would be rude. It's one thing to poke fun and make remarks on a subject that everyone knows isn't true. It's a whole other thing when it's true. Neither of them wanted to breach the subject first, for so many reasons. There was the obvious reason: never-ending ribbing. They could handle that. It was more the fear of perception. If they were a thing, would the others feel Ben and Nancy would let their relationship affect their work? It was a dangerous profession, after all. Would they tend to focus on the other's well-being over their duty to their team — that kind of bullshit? That type of thinking had stopped both of them on numerous opportune times from making a move.

"Okay, folks. Let's get back on track here. We've got a lot of ground to cover. We need to get this right." Captain Robertson's voice held a sense of urgency, and everyone sensed there was more to this fire than Robertson was letting on.

"The Kalispel Tribe contacted me this morning. They are especially concerned about this fire up on Hoodoo Mountain. Some kind of sacred land, or some shit like that. They are worried the 'Spirit of the Mountain' will be angry, and we don't need anything else trying to slow us down up there." There was some sarcasm in his voice, and a low chuckle passed through the group.

"All right, all right, I know. Evil spirits and shit. But these folks are serious, and we need to respect that. When you guys get to the forest service road, there will be a contingent of Kalispel shamans and elders. They want to bless you and offer protection to you guys from the Seatco.

It was pronounced *see-at-co*, and it was no joke to the Kalispel.

"Supposedly some kind of giant creature from a legend in their culture. I guess instead of the Boogeyman we should be afraid of the Seatco."

The folklore of the primitive Natives didn't deter the white man from coming. They just figured these poor, uneducated savages, like other ancient peoples, lifted animals to godlike status. Or, maybe, they made it up to try to scare them away. Either way, it didn't matter. Like many times throughout history, seeing was believing. After all, there wouldn't be so many stories of mysterious deaths, disappearances, and sightings if not for those who didn't heed the warnings.

Everyone got a good laugh from that. Everyone except Jackson Matoskah, whose last name roughly translated to *white bear*. Jack, as everyone called him, could trace his lineage all the way back to Chief Loyola, one of the most noted figures in Kalispel history. Jack's last name, "White Bear," could be traced to the legend of the Hoodoo.

The Hoodoo was said to be covered in white hair and able to take on the biggest grizzly bears. The last name was bestowed on his family by a tribal Shaman as a way to protect his family on hunts in the Hoodoo Mountain area. There were many tales passed down from grandfathers to fathers to sons over the decades — tales of eerie calls in the night, strange footprints in the earth and snow, and the disappearance of those who did not respect the mountain or the creatures who dwelled there.

Jack, himself, had an experience on the mountain while hunting. He never said anything to anyone. There was really nothing to tell — an eerie coincidence, a lucky break, or maybe something else. On a deer hunt in one of the drainages along Hoodoo Mountain, Jack had shot a large whitetail buck. While following the blood trail, Jack felt as though he was being watched but shrugged it off and pushed forward. He had tracked the deer for about 150 yards when he caught a glimpse of movement in the woods to his left and noticed a nasty odor in the air. Thinking he might have piqued the interest of a hungry bear, he kept one eye on the blood trail and one on the woods. About thirty yards ahead, he saw the white belly of his deer. It was down and dead, and Jack began his field dressing chore by thanking his ancestors and the Great Spirit for a successful hunt. Just as he started the gut the deer, he noticed movement to his right. Jack turned to face the intruder and saw he was face to face with a mountain lion. Not good. He had leaned his rifle up against a tree, and it was too far away to grab. The two stared each other down for what seemed like an eternity, and just when Jack figured it was going to get ugly, the cat suddenly turned and stared at the woods, where Jack thought a bear might be following from, looking for an easy meal. The large cat stared at the woods for about thirty seconds, then its body language completely changed to a submissive, almost scared, posture. Then it just turned and ran into the woods to the right and up the mountain. Jack immediately dashed for his rifle and turned to face the bear, only to see empty woods. No bear. Nothing but a pungent odor permeating the air. Jack got that nervous feeling in his chest. He went on completing the task at hand. He had never field dressed any animal as fast as that one, and just when he thought he was home free, the loudest, most bone-chilling scream pierced the woods, emanating from the bench just above him.

That was no mountain lion, he thought.

That's when he remembered the stories, and he felt nauseous. His heart began pounding so hard he thought it would explode, and adrenaline raced through his body. Normally, it would take Jack over an hour to pack out the meat and arrive at his truck. It only took thirty minutes that day. Could it have been the Hoodoo watching him? What was that smell? That scream... What animal made that noise? Jack shrugged it off as jitters from coming so close to the mountain lion. But after hearing Captain Robertson speak of spirits and Native legends, he wasn't so sure. Maybe there's something to this Hoodoo thing. He wasn't very active in his tribe, but he was happy they would be receiving a tribal blessing. Just in case.

"Hey, Jack. Aren't you Kalispel?" Nancy seemed anxious for a positive answer. Maybe she even felt there was something different about this mission. As a lifelong resident of Northern Idaho, she had heard the stories. She knew the legend, but it never really entered her mind. Until now.

Jackson was proud of his heritage but very much part of the

outside world. He had been to some tribal meetings and powwows but felt disconnected from the politics of the tribe. He grew up off the reservation, but his grandfather did his best to school Jackson in Kalispel tribal ways. One could say he was a man of two worlds. His mettle would be tested in the coming days in ways no one could prepare him for. Maybe his grandfather, a holy man in the tribe, knew Jackson would need the tribal knowledge he infused in his grandson.

"You know it, Mills. I'll be okay, but all you white guys are screwed." That brought a chuckle to the room.

"Well, Jack. Maybe you being on my team will give us some of that mojo. Sorry, Stumpy and Squatch. Been nice working with you." Gallows humor — the ability to laugh at death while facing the possibility of one's own demise. It was a prerequisite for any first-responder profession. Maybe that's what enabled them to run towards danger when everyone else was running away.

Everybody loaded their gear onto the trucks and piled in. There were four trucks, relics from the military; each could carry ten firefighters comfortably, as well as all their gear. Having four might be overkill with only twenty crew, but trucks break down or worse, and there weren't any repair shops in a working fire. Sometimes, the teams had to split into smaller groups and move quickly to different areas of a fire. The extra trucks could move crew and equipment around faster than walking, assuming drivable roads. The state had bought them at auction and refitted them for firefighting. Each truck had a hundred-gallon tank of drinking water and a food locker with enough canned goods and dehydrated rations to last three days. All the firefighting gear was stored in steel lockers mounted along the sides of the trucks. With the solid rubber tires, there would be no flat tires from all the rocky roads they drove. And they were six-wheel drive. To say the least, they were tanks.

It would take half an hour to get to the base of the mountain, and they were leaving late in the afternoon. It would be dark by the time the teams got into it. Normally, there would be ribbing and sassing each other back and forth. Not today. It was an unusually quiet drive.

The convoy of firefighters turned off of the Spirit Lake Cutoff Road and onto Clagstone Road. Not much farther to the forest service road.

"Holy shit! Have you ever seen such a sight?" Captain Robertson was in the lead vehicle and was the first to see the spectacle that awaited them at the forest service road. There were a dozen Kalispel tribal leaders in full ceremonial dress — feathers, deerskin garb, face paint, and drums. It was quite a sight. As the caravan approached the reception committee of elders, one man walked out from the group and motioned for the convoy to stop.

"Christ! Just what we need, a fuckin' party when we've got a damn fire to fight." Captain Robertson was not happy, but protocol and politics creates uncomfortable allowances. Robertson didn't place much stock in this hocus-pocus bullshit, but he had to respect the will of the locals.

Robertson radioed to the other trucks and told them to hang tight until he found out what was what. When he stepped out of the truck, he was greeted by Jimmy Two Horns, a shaman and a respected leader in the local community, not just the Kalispel Tribe. Jimmy was known for his uncanny ability to know someone's true nature, whether someone was trustworthy or not, honest or a lying, cheating son of a bitch. He looked into Captain Robertson's eyes, waved a smoking sage-stuffed roll around Robertson's face, stuck his finger in the ash of the roll, and stroked it across Robertson's forehead. He was performing the time-honored tradition of "smudging." It was supposed to ward off evil and offer protection. Two Horns mumbled something in Kalispel that Robertson couldn't understand. Then he leaned into Robertson's left ear and whispered, "You will be tested. You will need to be pure of purpose. I pray that the Spirit of the Mountain will see your nature and spare you and your people."

What kind of crap was *that*? Spirit of the Mountain... Right. Robertson was about to laugh, but Two Horns added an ominous warning.

"Do not doubt the warnings of the people. Not all of you will return from this mountain. There will be death, and it will not all be from fire. Four trucks in, two trucks out. There are things you do not understand, but you will. The Seatco will seek payment."

Robertson saw something in Two Horn's eyes that made him feel as though he knew something. Not that he thought something might happen, but that he *knew* it would. Like he had already seen it happen, and there would be no way to change it.

Robertson leaned back and uttered a quick thank-you, then headed back to the truck.

"All right, ladies. Break's over. Let's get to work." He was anxious to get to work and focus on the job at hand instead of what Jimmy Two Horn had said. He got a slight chill down his spine, and he could only hope Two Horns was full of shit, but something told him to be on guard.

As each truck passed the Kalispel elders, Jimmy Two Horns waived the smoking sage roll over them while chanting the ritual blessing for protection. His gaze was focused skyward until the truck with Jackson Matoskah passed by. At the very moment Jack reached Two Horns, Two Horns dropped his eyes and stared directly into Jackson's. It was as if Jimmy could sense Jack's presence in the truck, and Jack felt as though Jimmy was talking directly to him. Jack couldn't quite make out what Jimmy was saying, except for one word. It almost jumped out at him.

"Seatco."

He could see something in Two Horn's eyes. Fear. What did he know? Were the stories his father and grandfather told him true? Was there something on this mountain that they should worry about? He shook it off as just tribal superstition. But, still, there was his own experience on this mountain during his hunt. He did feel as if something was there. Watching.

"Hey, Jack, what's eatin' ya?" Steve Parsons was sitting next to Jack and could see his far-off stare.

"Hmm? Oh, nothing, SP. I was just remembering a deer hunt up on this mountain a few years ago. Good hunting up here."

3

SENTRY

It was watching. High up on a hidden rock outcrop. It always watched the mountain. It had to. It's what its kind have always done. Yes, its kind. There are more than one; there has to be for it to have been talked about for hundreds of years. But there weren't many of them — small groups scattered all over the world. A throwback to a time before written history. They have seen the comings and goings of species, of wilderness, of the balance of natural things. They were somewhere between animal and man. Not a missing link, but more a missing species. When the tribes of man first appeared on the land, they were there, watching. The ancient humans were more in tune with their surroundings. More in touch with the sensitive balance of all species. They honored life and death, and those who watched them respected them.

There are numerous stories in almost every Native American tribe about encounters between the people and what they called the secret or lost tribe — a tribe of wild men that were neither man nor animal. They were very tall, hairy, extremely strong, and did not tolerate trespassers. There are accounts of them tossing 200-pound boulders down on anyone who got too close. Mostly, those were thrown as a warning, landing just close enough to get the attention of the trespassers to deter them from venturing any farther. Mostly, they threw smaller stones — egg- or softball-size rocks. Those were readily available and could be thrown from much greater distances, enabling the thrower to stay hidden, adding to the mystery and fear of them. When warnings failed to halt the incursions, they would not hesitate to stop the intruders by other means. There are many stories of hunting parties that never returned to camp after presumably wandering into the forbidden territories.

Over time, as people came from other countries and the desire for animal pelts and pristine land grew, the secret tribe was forced to retreat to more and more rugged and remote environs in order to survive. The shear ruggedness of their lands kept most people away. They would limit the size of their groups to help keep them hidden.

Each group mostly kept to itself, getting together with other groups only in times of great threat or when it came time to breed. The group, or tribe, was primarily made up of blood relatives. This meant none of them would breed with any other in the group. This kept the hierarchy of the group mostly unchallenged; it only became an issue upon the death of the alpha. When one of them died, disposing of the body fell to the omega group member. This assured that each member of the group had a purpose, which in turn helped keep order. The omega would take the body off to be dismembered, and the body parts were scattered about the mountain so that nature's cleanup crew could do its part to hide any evidence of the group's existence. They didn't use tools; they were so powerfully built that they would pull the body apart, like pulling apart chicken. It is said coyotes developed a particular bond with these creatures. They would follow them at a distance where they could safely feed off the tribe's scraps. There were always scraps to be had, and the coyotes would drag body parts back to their dens to feed new litters of pups. This, effectively, served to bury the bones and further hide any evidence. If bones were found by outsiders, they were not usually intact and thus often misidentified as parts of large ungulates, such as elk or moose. Most who came across these remnants never gave them a second look. This would explain why no one ever found a carcass or skeleton of the creatures. After all, bears are well-known animals, yet not many bear carcasses are found in the forest. Nothing goes to waste in the natural world.

Over time, they even developed a non-verbal way of communicating over long distances by hitting trees with branches or rocks to create various "knocks." Outsiders would think the sounds were just rocks falling or other natural sounds in the woods. When they did vocalize, their ally, the coyote, would join in by yipping and howling. This disguised the creature's call. It wasn't always successful, though. Some people have heard the calls and knocks and seen the tracks. Tracks were usually left because the creature made a hasty retreat of was too focused on hunting prey. Most of the time, they stayed off soft ground, choosing rocky areas where tracks were less obvious.

These creatures — or beings, as they more accurately should be called — have an intelligence — not human intelligence, but they are able to reason some things out. They are smart enough to stay out of sight and not leave much evidence of their existence, so that those who claim to see one are usually laughed at, ridiculed, and not taken seriously. But they are real. They watch everything around them and will protect their ever-shrinking lands. As they have always done, they leave little or no evidence of violence, if possible.

They do have one give-away, one "tell," in gambling parlance. They smell, and they smell *bad*. Their odor comes from a combination of natural musk, used in attracting a mate, and the remnants of the prey left in their hair. Meals usually consist of fish and and other small game, like squirrels or rabbits. As well, they forage from abundant huckleberry bushes and other edible plants in great supply along the high ridges and fertile valleys of their lands. Their size and strength are immense; some are over ten feet tall. They are fully capable of stalking and killing large game, like deer or even elk. Though not a rare event, hunting larger game is limited. The larger the animal, the more opportunity for injury. Where they live is hard country, and a bad enough injury can result in a prolonged death. Most sightings of these beings are credited to injured ones. The theory is that the injury forces them to look for easier food sources:

vegetable gardens, fruit trees, chicken coops, goats, pigs. Anything they can get to without too much exertion. In some tribes, it was known as the "one who steals food." Could it be that those were injured ones, too weak to catch their own food? Theories are all over the board when there is so little evidence of their existence.

But, for now, it sits. Watching. Watching the trucks as they wind up the dirt road that leads to its lair. It could smell the exhaust fumes, even through the smoke from the ever-growing fire on its land. It could smell the sweat pouring off these humans and could smell the fear it contained. It couldn't know that these humans were there to help. The closer they got to its home, the angrier it got. It had already punished the two that started the fire on its homeland, and it was willing to do so again. Just as its kind had always done. Protect the lands, protect itself, and protect the group. A seemingly simple doctrine, but there were other considerations. Its group needed food, and the fire was reducing its primary food sources. It might have to seek food from the lands below, and then return to its mountain. But, for now, it would watch. The sun was setting and this was its prime time.

They had exceptional sight in the dark. They were holdouts from prehistoric times and actually made their own "eye-shine." Eye-shine usually occurs when light strikes the eyes of an animal. It's a result of the back of their eyes being covered with what is called tapetum lucidum. Suffice it to say, it makes eyes glow when light hits it. But it's different with these beings. It's as if they make their eyes actually glow with a luminescence. It appears that light is not needed to react with the tapetum. But, in fact, it's more similar to night vision technology than magic. Their eyes magnify ambient light to maximize their ability to see in the dark. Night was falling and they ruled the night. Although having the ability to see pretty well in the dark, their vision did change from a full range of colors to shades of black, grey, and white. Even with the limited color spectrum, it was extremely crisp and it allowed them to move quickly through the night. Most of their hunting was at night as that's when most of their food was active.

4

FIRST CONTACT

It was a fourteen-mile drive up twisty, bumpy, dusty, pothole-filled dirt road. Driving at a snail's pace, it took the convoy of five trucks almost an hour to reach the jump-off point. They could see the glow of the fire in the valley below, even through the ever-thickening smoke moving uphill towards their vehicles.

"This is ground zero, people. Get your gear, and get your heads in the game!" Captain Robertson approached every fire like a coach strategizing against a foe hellbent on burning everything it comes in contact with. They always started on defense, but the plan was to get on offense as quickly as possible.

"Stumpy and Squatch, take your trucks down this feeder road. It's running about a mile or so above the fire. Get your teams down there and see if you can widen that road up a bit to slow the fire down. Mills, get your team up to the east above that ridge, up on grid II-A. There's a firebreak up there and an avalanche slide that's mostly boulders. Rocks don't burn, so if the fire closes in on you guys, you should have enough time to hunker down in the rocks until the fire moves past you. Let's hope that doesn't happen. I'm counting on your team to get some firebreaks cut in so we can buy some time and get ahead of this thing. Once the breaks are cut, I want your team to light some back-burns. If it gets past you, the town of Spirit Lake is within striking distance. With any luck, and if the winds don't change, maybe we can get this bastard under control. Sorry, but this terrain is too steep for the dozers. It's gonna be all manpower."

If at all possible, fire crews prefer to use bulldozers or other heavy equipment to clear vast areas of underbrush and other materials that could provide fuel for a fire. Not only was this area steep, it was full of granite outcrops and large boulders. Bulldozers would just get bogged down and become a liability. At least the crews could move reasonably fast over this topography, and that's just what was needed. Speed. The fire started on a small foothill below Hoodoo Mountain and had to burn downhill first. Fires typically burn downhill at a slower pace than when they burn uphill.

The predicted winds hadn't hit yet, giving the fire teams a huge break. Wind moves a fire much faster than when left to its own devices, which is plenty fast enough on its own. The other good news was the fire started on the western aspect, or face, of the mountain. The predicted winds were to come in from the south. The town of Spirit Lake was to the north, south, and east of the fire, meaning the winds would push the fire away from town. But fire seems to have a way of moving however it damn well wants to, so speed was the name of the game, and Nancy's team was the right tool for the job. They moved *fast*. They were a thorough group, but they left other teams in the dust. They were in great physical condition. They would need it; this mountain was steep on all sides. If the fire made it to Hoodoo Mountain, it would climb so fast, no one would have a change to get out of the way. As said in firefighter circles, they would become crispy critters. That was no way to go.

Nancy and her crew made it to their jump-off point. It was very smokey, and the fire at the bottom gave the forest an eerie orange glow. It was just past sunset, but they could see well enough to start with the chainsaws.

"Okay, boys, let's get to work. Jack, you and Wilson get started on this side clearing those trees. SP, take Spud with you and get to the drainage on the other side of this slide. Get that flank cleared, and let me know as soon as you're ready, and we'll get those burns started.

Jack and Dave Wilson were the best tree fellers, or sawyers, on the crew, maybe the whole forest fire service. They competed in chainsaw events at the area logging competitions. Although most participants were in the logging industry, these competitions were open to anyone with a chainsaw, and Jack and Dave were always a threat to win. This made them a valuable team in cutting fire breaks. They were fast, accurate, and safe. No one wanted to lose a limb or have a tree fall on them. Especially with a forest fire in the mix.

Steve Parsons, or SP, and Spud were also adept at the chainsaw. Spud, whose real name was Brian Frye, was from British Columbia, Canada and spoke some French. Initially, he was called French Frye, but it was later shortened to Spud. Spud was a little loose with the chainsaw. Where the team of Jackson and Wilson could drop trees within inches of their targeted direction, Spud and SP used direction as more of a guideline. Trees fell in mostly the right direction, but there were more occurrences of hang-ups, or trees that got hung up on a nearby tree. Although they were fast, they spent more time un-fouling trees. This is why they usually were sent to the far side of the fire line, where there was less chance of slowing the rest of the team down. They made up for their mishaps by being the two fastest members of Team C. Maybe the fastest members of this or any fire platoon. Everyone had their strengths and weaknesses, and a good leader knew how to get the most out of each person's strengths while minimizing their weaknesses. Nancy Mills was an expert at this, and it's one thing that made her such a good leader. It didn't hurt that she got just as dirty, just as tired, and just as physical as each member of the team — LBX, or leadership by example, as she called it. That was the only way to be when everyone's life is on the line. Everyone dies alone, and there is no difference in death. Rookie, veteran, team leader, professional, or volunteer — they could each die a terrible death if anyone drops the ball. Every person on the team knew this. Every person on the team accepted this. And every person on the team lived by the code: protect the person on either side; they are all you have. They are family.

Nancy and the rest of the crew started cutting a firebreak between the two teams falling trees. It's a delicate dance between crashing trees, smoke, heat, and removing anything that the fire might use as fuel. One of the sneakiest things a fire does is what some firefighters call a fuse. It's when fire burns along a tree's root system underground. This type of fire is almost impossible to see, and if a root system goes under a fire break to the other side and finds a source of fuel, it could trap the teams between two fires. For this reason, Nancy and her team were digging deep to try to cut off any "fuses" before they become a problem — hard work on sloped and rocky terrain.

While Mills' team worked to form the higher firebreaks, Stumpy and Squatch started their teams on widening the spur road. These roads were cut in by logging companies so they could remove their timber without always having to haul trees up to one location. This cut down on fuel, time, and man hours, thereby increasing profits. Using spur roads wasn't always an option, but when able to, they did. They also made great access roads for fire teams, so fire service maps were updated periodically so teams knew if there were spur roads in the area and what condition they might be in. This spur road was about ten years old and had some areas where chaparral, alders, and other low-growing shrubs had overtaken the access. These roads become highways for game animals such as deer, moose, and elk, because they offered both cover and a relatively easy way to move around the mountain.

"Holy shit! That fuckin' moose almost slammed right into our truck."

Proctor didn't see the moose until it was almost on top of him. It was dark, the smoke obscured visibility, and the damn things were dark brown.

"Fire's got the critters on the move, so watch your asses out there, boys, or you might get stomped."

There was no real danger of getting stomped, and everyone knew it. It was just a mood lightener, a way to ease some tension, because things were heating up, and it wasn't just the fire.

"Gotta stop and clear this chaparral, Squatch." Mike Nelson was driving the forest service truck with Proctor's team.

"Okay, boys, looks like we start here." Proctor hopped of the truck and ran back to the other truck carrying Stumpy's team.

"Hey, Stumpy, we're gonna clear this shit out of the way and start our clear-cutting here. Once this section of road is opened, get your team on down about half a mile or so and do the same. We'll work toward each other and meet in the middle."

Stumpy got his crew out of the trucks to help clear the road.

"Time to get dirty, guys."

It didn't take long for the two teams of twenty to clear thirty yards of underbrush, and Stumpy's team was soon headed to their starting point. The lights from his truck faded almost instantly with the amount of smoke pouring up the mountain. It gave Proctor a chill to see Stumpy's truck disappear like that. Almost like the Mountain swallowed him up.

Stumpy's team was a little over a mile from Proctor's team when — *bam*!

"What the hell was that?"

Stumpy's truck reeled from being struck by something. Something *big*. The truck actually lurched to the left.

"Stop the truck! Let me check it out."

Larry Carter was driving this truck. He was a twelve-year veteran and familiar with this spur road.

"Felt like we got hit by somethin'. Somethin' *big*. Steerin's kinda outta whack, too."

Stumpy went out to the front end to see what happened.

"Damn it! Carter, take a look at this!"

"What ya got, boss?"

"We got nailed by a damn boulder. I think your rim's bent, and that damn rock's wedged in the wheel well. We don't have time to fuck with it, now. Bad luck. Just plain bad luck. I guess we're walking the rest of the way. It's not much farther to our target, so grab the gear.

"Well;" said Carter, "if you can spare me for about an hour, I think I can use one of the push poles to free the truck from the boulder. I can drive a short bit with a bent rim, and we ain't gonna go very fast, anyway. I'll meet you guys up the way in an hour or so. What do ya' say?"

Stumpy didn't like leaving anyone alone during a fire. Safety dictated someone stay with him.

"Okay, Carter. But I'm leaving Slim with you. You could use the extra hand, and maybe you can cut the time in half."

"Okay, boss. Sounds good."

Paul Garret, aka Slim, was six feet four inches tall and only weighed 175 pounds. He was skinny. Hard to get pants to fit a thirty-one-inch waist with a thirty-six-inch inseam. But he was one of those strong, wiry kids. Hard to slow him down. Even though he had only been on the team for two years, he had the abilities of a much more seasoned pro. Slim and Carter started to work on getting the truck loose from the boulder as Stumpy and the rest of the team hoofed it up the spur road to start work on widening it into a decent firebreak.

"Damn! This rock is wedged in *tight*." Carter was working at using the push pole as a lever. The solid steel pole, about eight feet long and a couple inches in diameter, was for rolling large logs and other debris out of the way.

Bam!

"Holy shit! That rock almost hit us." Slim was just moving to a different position to help Carter leverage the push pole, when the softball-size rock slammed into the front passenger door, leaving a sizable dent and nearly hitting Slim in the shoulder.

"We're in a bad place, Carter. We need to get this damn truck—" *Bam!* "*Another* one? That one almost took your head off, Carter. We better get our hard hats before one of us gets our head stove in."

That second rock was about the same size and landed on the hood of the truck, missing Carter's nose by an inch.

"You're right, Slim. I almost caught that one in the snozz!"

Carter and Slim ran to the back of the truck to retrieve their hard hats, when a third rock struck the truck. This time, it hit the back quarter panel a foot from where the two men had just moved to.

"What the fuck is going on? It's almost like someone is purposely trying to hit us with those damn rocks. Is there a loose boulder field above us? I don't like it." Carter was nervous. They both felt as if someone or some*thing* was throwing these rocks, and if that was the case, they would be sitting ducks while they worked on freeing the truck.

Bam! Bam! Crash!

Those three rocks hit in virtually the same spot on the door as the first rock that hit the door, and the third rock crashed through that door's window.

Slim looked up where the rocks were coming from. All he could see was darkness and smoke. Straining his eyes to scan the night for their assailant was futile. Whoever or whatever was tossing rocks at them was too far away for them to see.

"Put your back into it, Carter! I think we're screwed if we don't get the hell out of here. I'm gonna radio ahead and tell Stumpy what's going on."

Slim made a mad dash to the driver's side door to get on the shortwave radio. He had just started to lift the door handle when the next rock hit. This one caught Slim on the right shoulder, throwing him backwards to the ground. His collarbone was broken, his shoulder was badly smashed up, and he hit his head hard on the door's window frame, knocking him senseless for a few seconds.

Adrenaline had surged through Carter's body, and he'd somehow shifted the truck off the boulder about the same time Slim got hit.

"Stay down! I'm comin' to ya'." Carter dropped to the ground and scurried on all fours to the driver's side.

Bam! Another rock hit the truck, but it would have hit Carter square in the head if he hadn't dropped to the ground so fast. Carter got to Slim and helped him into the back cab floorboard.

"Stay on the floor on this side of the truck. You got more protection there."

Slim was bleeding badly and in a lot of pain. His right shoulder was useless. As Carter moved towards the driver's seat, lifting his head above the floorboards, he could see through the broken passenger window and a little ways up the slope above them. That's when he thought he caught a glimpse of something. Something *huge*. It was moving from right to left, about fifty yards up the mountain. He only even caught a glimpse of it because it was white — solid white — and reflected the firelight glow far below. It had moved fast and disappeared into the dark almost as soon as Carter saw it.

Carter had no time to ponder what he saw. He had to get this truck moving and up the road to the others. After all, there was safety in numbers, right?

It saw the humans exiting their trucks. It watched as they started cutting down its trees and destroying the low brush that offered so much cover for its movements and provided ambush spots when it hunted. They were killing its home, and they had to be stopped. It watched as the trucks split and went separate ways. It waited for the right time to strike. A single truck moved along the road, and darkness was falling. The time was close. The bend in the road was a pinch point — a narrow part of the road that was open to the bench above where it watched from. It would be easy to stop the truck, and then stop the humans. The boulder was in the perfect spot to roll onto the road and into the truck. It wouldn't take much effort; it had moved much larger boulders to block access into its land.

The boulder struck the truck perfectly and wouldn't be able to be moved before it could eliminate the threat to its home.

It waited until there weren't so many people — easier to fight a smaller number than to take on so many at once. It would use the night and its strength to kill these threats from afar. It had used this technique many times in hunting. It would stun its food with a rock then move in close to break the neck. A clean kill. Killing humans was easier. A well-placed rock throw should do it. It hadn't counted on the smoke, though. Smoke made it more difficult to see the target. They saw in shades of black, gray, and white. Smoke encompassed all those shades, so it acted as camouflage. It obscured the humans from sight, affecting its rock-throwing accuracy, fortunately for Slim and Carter. Not only were they partially hidden from the creature because of the smoke; they were moving, and moving targets were always more difficult, even without smoke.

It had only placed enough rocks at this sight to accomplish its mission. After missing the humans on the first volley, it shifted position to gain a better vantage where the smoke was less a factor. This placed it within view of the humans, but they would be dead soon, so it wouldn't be a problem. It hadn't counted on both of them moving to the protected side of the truck, but it was able to knock one of them down with a well-placed throw. It was out of rocks now and moving to collect more, when the second human moved and started the truck. When the truck moved down the road, it let out a call to summon help from the rest of its group. If they were to save their lands, the whole group would need to engage.

"Did you hear that? Holy shit! What the hell kinda' animal sounds like that?" As Carter turned the key in the ignition, a loud, guttural howl emitted from where he'd seen the creature. He breathed a short sigh of relief when the truck's engine started up right away.

Slim was sprawled out on the floorboards in the back of the cab. The rock had virtually crushed his shoulder, and he was in severe pain. The howl snapped him out of his pain-induced fog, and he tried to sit up.

"Oh, crap! I can't use my left arm, at all. What's going on, Carter? Who could throw rocks that size, that hard, and that accurate?"

Nobody, thought Carter. He couldn't get the vision of that creature out of his head, but he had a job to do. He grabbed the radio handset. "Sam. Come in, Sam! This is Carter. Pick up, Sam!" He was almost yelling into the mic.

"Sam?" Stumpy knew something was up. No one ever called him Sam. It was always Stumpy.

"What's up, Carter? What you got?"

"We're coming in fast. Slim's hurt bad, and he needs to be evacuated. We need a chopper in here. The truck's not going to make it back down the mountain with the wheel all busted up. Keep your damn eyes open, Sam. Something's in these woods I ain't never seen before, and it's what hurt Slim. It's big. *Very* big."

Stumpy could hear the fear in Carter's voice, and he had heard a strange animal sound from their general direction. He thought it might have been a cougar, even though it didn't quite sound like one. He tried to shrug off Carter's fear as nerves caused by the eerie orange fire glow dancing in the smoke. It gave the night a strange, almost other-worldly feel. That said, Stumpy couldn't help but look up the mountain for whatever Slim and Carter encountered. He felt an uneasiness creep over him. He looked over at his team. They had all stopped their work after hearing Carter's radio call and were looking at Stumpy. He had never seen that look on his men's faces before. It was fear. Primal, instinctual, basic fear.

"What's happening, Stumpy? What was Carter talkin' about? Sounded like some kind of monster or somethin'." This was Craig Stephens' first fire, and he was already pretty nervous.

Stumpy looked at Craig and tried to sound casual. "Oh, you know Carter. Probably tryin' to get a rise out of you rookies. He'll fly up in here, and Slim will be all hunched over just waiting for one of us to rush to help. They'll get a big laugh out of it, and we'll get our asses back to work."

"Hope you're right, boss. But he sure sounded sacred to me."

Stumpy thought the same thing, but he was responsible for this group and wasn't going to jump to conclusions. For all he knew, a bear or something scurrying away from the fire below just knocked some debris loose, and it just happened to hit Slim. Right. Happened all the time, but for now, he would wait until Carter and Slim got here to evaluate. In the meantime, he had a firebreak to cut and an air ambulance to call. It was common practice to have one or two air assets, usually helicopters, located close to the fire zone. They could be used at a moment's notice to provide water drops on the fire or air ambulance service in case of injured firefighters, like Slim. This saved time, thereby saving lives.

"Captain. Did you copy Carter on that chopper for Slim?"

Captain Robertson had heard the call go out on the radio and was already on the horn to central command.

"Ten-four, Sam. Got a chopper on the way, but you're gonna have to get Slim up to that logging helipad about two clicks from your position. It's the only spot open and level enough for the chopper."

"Roger that, Captain. Out."

"Keep me in the loop on what's goin' on, up there."

"Ten-four, Captain."

Nancy Mills and her crew overheard the radio transmission too. They were about a mile up from Stumpy and his team and had a fully functional truck.

"Hey, Stumpy, we're not too far from ya', and our truck's in good shape. You want me to send someone down to shuttle Slim? We could be there in about ten or fifteen minutes."

"Negative, Mills. I'll get Proctor to run them up. He's closer."

"Roger that."

Proctor was already putting a plan in motion to intercept Carter and Slim.

"I got a truck on the way to you, Stumpy. Might even catch your guys." Hey, Moore, get Toothless and take the truck down to Stumpy!"

Jesse Moore was a good choice for this. He was the best medic on the team, and Frank Welch, aka Toothless, was just plain strong. He once carried an injured firefighter and his gear two miles without a break. Stopping would've meant death by fire. He got his nickname from his missing front tooth, which was knocked out when he was a teenager playing baseball. A fast pitch hit him square in the mouth while he was at bat. The story goes, he just spit the tooth out and kept playing. He wouldn't even let his parents get it fixed. He said it made him look tougher.

"On it, Boss."

Just as the lights from Moore and Toothless' truck disappeared around a turn, another loud howling echoed through the woods. This one came from above the spur road and close to Nancy's team. It stopped Nancy mid-stride, and she felt the fearful chill of unease. She had heard a similar sound to her left and below, but it was hard to make out with all the chainsaw and equipment racket. This one, however, was *very* clear and unlike anything she'd heard before, but as the only woman out there, she wasn't about to let the fellas see her rattled. She just pretended she hadn't heard a thing and went back to work. But she had, in fact, heard it, and she couldn't stop her brain from pondering what it was. And just when she thought she might get away with ignoring it, another howl pierced the air. This one was a different pitch and was from her right. No ignoring this one. Everyone on the team heard it and all stopped what they were doing and looked at Nancy to see what she would do.

"I don't have a clue, guys. Something is out there making that noise, and I think it's more than one. Pair up! No one goes off on their own. I don't care if you gotta pee. You pee, your buddy pees with you. Got it? I'm grabbing the team shotgun, and I'll keep an eye out for anything out of the ordinary."

Each truck had a twelve-gauge shotgun mounted in the cab. It was there in case of emergencies, usually to dispatch injured animals. Having the shotgun made Nancy feel a little better, but she wished there was more than one.

Everyone got it. Even though that howl had them rattled, they still had a job to do, and they were going to do it or die trying.

Moore and Toothless got to Team C's location about the same time Carter and Slim arrived.

Carter jumped out of the truck and was white as a ghost, like he was in shock.

"Somethin's out there. It tried to kill us. Look at the fuckin' truck! It's smashed all to hell.

Slim's hurt pretty bad, but he's awake. We gotta get him outta here. We all gotta get outta here. Did you hear them howls? They're all over the damn mountain."

Carter was ranting so fast, he was almost incoherent.

"Calm down, Carter! Help Toothless get Slim in the other truck. Chopper's on its way, and we need to get him up to that helipad just a couple miles up the road. We have a job to do, and no stinkin' ghost is gonna stop us."

"Stumpy, I *saw* the damn thing. It's fuckin' *huge*. It's covered all over in hair. White hair. It threw those damn rocks at us and just about killed us. It's after us, and we ain't gotta chance. We got one damn shotgun per truck, and I don't think that's enough."

"All right, Carter. Go get some water and take a seat for a minute. Let me try to figure something out."

Moore and Toothless were helping Slim to the other truck.

"Carter's right, Stumpy. That thing was throwing pretty damn big rocks a long damn way, *and* it was fucking accurate. I didn't see it like Carter did, but I smelled it. It stinks."

Moore got Slim's shoulder immobilized by tying his arm down with the ace bandages from the first aid kit.

"This will keep you from making your shoulder any worse. Lots of tendons and crap in there. Just sit as still as you can, and we'll get you outta here."

The road to the helipad wasn't really a road. It was a dragline designed to pull logs up to the helipad by using cables and pulleys. It was barely wide enough for the truck and was bumpy and over-grown, but it was the quickest way there. Speed was key, not just because Slim's injury was bad, but because they still had a fire to fight.

"Holy shit! You gotta hit *every* damn bump?" The adrenaline was wearing off, and Slim felt every jolt in his shoulder.

"Easy, Slim. I can see the chopper approaching the landing pad. It's not too far now." Moore was trying to keep Slim calm. Shock could hit an injured person any time and turn a non-life-threatening injury life-threatening in a hurry.

Nancy's team was working with a purpose. Everyone was both clearing underbrush and looking over their shoulders for whatever Carter was rambling on about.

"I'm tellin' ya', Nancy. There's something out here with us, and it's bad news." Carter was pacing and looking up the mountain, half expecting to see "it" rise up at any moment.

"Take a breath, Carter! Jesus! You're freakin' everyone out. I've hiked these mountains all my life and never seen any evidence of *anything* like you say you saw. You're just letting shadows or something mess with your head. Probably saw an albino bear or something." Nancy was making sure *all* her crew heard her. She wanted to calm the team down so they could focus on the job at hand — fighting fires. Truth be told, though, she was also trying to convince herself there was some other explanation for what Slim and Carter had encountered. It wasn't working. She was more nervous and edgier than when she'd taken her first fire crew into the field. There were no manuals for this.

The rescue helicopter was approaching the landing pad, and the truck carrying Slim was almost there.

"Hit the floods." The pilot, Rick Matthews, needed all the light he could get to make sure he cleared any obstacles. Between the smoke and the debris his rotors were kicking up, it was hard to get a clear understanding of the terrain. Copilot Sean Lebsok hit the switches, and the landing area flooded with bright light that extended in all directions and up the mountain about a hundred feet.

"Did you see that, Rick? As soon as I hit the lights, something huge darted off through that pine thicket. Looked like it was all white or something."

"Probably a moose. Those spots are so bright, they tend to wash the color out of anything they shine on."

I'm tellin' you, it wasn't no moose. It had arms."

Matthews wasn't buying it. Either Lebsok was messing with him, or the smoke and shadows were playing tricks on his eyes.

"All right, Sean. Here comes our passenger. Let's see what we got."

As soon as the chopper touched down, Moore, Toothless, and Slim pulled up to the landing area.

Lebsok ran over with a stretcher and looked Slim over. "Hey, fellas. That was good timing. Doesn't get much better than that." Lebsok checked Slim's vitals and made sure his injury was wrapped up tight for the flight into Newport General Hospital, in Newport, Washington. It would be a fifteen-minute flight from Hoodoo Mountain. "All right, looking good. Let's get him to the chopper."

Lebsok and Toothless stretchered Slim into the helicopter. Once there, it was another few minutes for IV hookup and strapping Slim in, and then they were off. Toothless moved just out of the way and ducked down with his eyes closed to protect them from flying debris. As soon as the helicopter cleared the treetops, Lebsok flipped off the spots, and they were inbound to Newport.

Moore had taken cover behind the truck as Lebsok and Toothless made their way to the chopper — better protection from all the flying trash there. With all the noise from the helicopter, Jesse Moore never heard it creep up closer. By the time he felt something wasn't quite right, it was too late. It grabbed him with its powerful arms and snapped Jesse's neck like a twig. Jesse never knew what hit him. It pulled his lifeless body into the thicket and up the mountain.

Toothless didn't hear anything, and he sure didn't see anything. As with any night operation, once the eyes are exposed to light, it takes about thirty minutes to fully re-adjust to the dark. And with the brightness of the spotlights, it would take Toothless a little longer. As the helicopter faded into the smokey night sky, Toothless was stumbling back to the truck, almost blind from the sudden darkness once the lights went out.

"Damn! Hey, Moore! Turn on the headlights. Moore! Moore? Jesse! Where the hell are you hiding?"

Toothless got to the truck and grabbed his flashlight stored in the door's side pocket. He flipped on the flashlight but didn't see Moore anywhere. As Toothless approached the back of the truck, he could see some blood spattered on the bumper and the ground, but no Jesse Moore. There were a couple of marks in the dirt that looked as if something had been dragged off into the woods. Suddenly, Toothless felt completely alone and, for the first time in as long as he could remember, he was truly scared. For just a few seconds, he froze in place, unable to get his head around what was going on. Then the smell hit his senses. It snapped him out of his daze as if someone had opened smelling salts under his nose. It was pungent and strong. All he could think about was Slim going on and on about some kind of huge creature and the awful smell when this thing attacked, and the blood on the truck. He knew he had to get out of there. He knew

Moore was probably badly hurt, or worse. But he also knew he couldn't leave his comrade on this mountain if there was any chance he was still alive. He had to make sure, so he grabbed the shotgun from the truck and, with great trepidation, followed the trail of blood and snapped branches up the mountain.

"Squatch, this is Toothless. Come in!" He knew he had to get word to the crews what he was doing and where he was heading in case something happened to him; they might know where to look.

"Go ahead, Toothless. Is Slim okay?"

"Ten-four, boss, but..." He hesitated while trying to come up with words to express what was happening. "Moore's gone. Just *gone.*"

Robertson could tell Toothless was rattled, and that was not normal. "Gone? What do you mean, gone?"

"He's gone, sir. I came back to the truck after they took off with Slim, and Moore was nowhere. Just some blood on the truck. Looks like something dragged him off into the woods. I'm gonna look for him. Out."

Robertson didn't need firefighters scattered all over the mountain. If the fire were to take a bad turn, they could be trapped up there.

"Negative, Welch. You get your ass in that truck and get back down here. We'll work out a plan from here."

Toothless ignored Robertson. His friend needed help, if he was still alive, and he knew Moore would do the same for him. Toothless started to track Moore's trail. He was slow and methodical, partly because the trail was hard to follow and partly — well, mostly — because his legs were shaking from fear. And what the hell was that damn smell?

After it killed Moore, it knew to hide the corpse. It would let the scavengers have the bounty. As it carried the body up the mountain, it would stop to sever body parts and toss them into the woods. By the time it had reached the cover of its home, a vast cave system that meandered through the mountain, it had discarded Moore's body across the wooded and boulder-strewn mountainside. In just a few days, the flesh, muscles, and organs would be gone. Birds and coyotes, mostly — nothing went to waste in nature. In a few weeks, larger predators along with the coyotes would have severed the bones and carried them off to dens or other safe places to gnaw on the marrow. Nothing went to waste. If any parts were found, it would most likely be years from now, and there wouldn't be enough evidence to determine the cause of death. This was how its kind had hidden evidence of their presence since their arrival long before recorded time.

Toothless was following the trail it had left. It wasn't hard to follow, even in the low light and smoke. Blood was everywhere. He knew his mission was futile. Toothless came to a more open area where he could see at least fifty feet around him. That's where the large blood pool was. It was a lot of blood, enough to determine Jesse Moore was probably dead. But there was something else. It wasn't really a footprint, but an outline of a foot created by Moore's blood splashing over the foot of whatever killed him. The print was almost complete; all but the heel area was outlined. Even if Welch didn't include the heel, the foot was monstrous. He put his foot inside the outline and estimated the print was five inches longer than his size-twelve boot. That's when he really felt alone. He took off running back down the mountain as fast as he could. He knew he didn't stand a chance up there alone. He reached the truck, battered and bruised from branches and stumbling down the mountain.

Captain Robertson had picked up two men from Team B to go with him to find out what was going on with Toothless and Moore. Brian Pitts and Mark Anderson were both ex-army who had seen combat in Iraq. They were with Robertson when Toothless got to the truck.

"Holy shit, Toothless! What the hell happened here? Where's Moore?"

Toothless was trying to tell them what he saw between gasps of air after his mad dash down the mountain.

"It (*gasp*) killed him! Took him (*gasp*) up there (*gasp*). I found a (gasp) footprint. (*Gasp, gasp, gasp.*) It was bigger than my (*gasp*) foot (*gasp*) by a *lot*. (*Gasp, gasp*). No Moore (*gasp*). Just lots of blood. (*Gasp, gasp*). We gotta get outta here!"

Everyone just stood there, trying to comprehend what they just heard. Robertson was first to ask what they were all thinking.

"How do you know Moore's dead? Did you find a body? Is it possible he's still alive up there?"

Toothless just stared blankly at Robertson. "No... No way he's alive. Too much blood. So much blood."

"Okay, guys, let's get back down to our crews. We'll put a plan together for how we proceed, but there's still a fire burning, and it's not waiting for anything."

Robertson and Toothless took one truck, and Pitts and Anderson took the other. Robertson and Toothless didn't say much. Toothless just stared out the window with that glazed-over look. Pitts and Anderson were quiet at first. Then Anderson started telling Pitts a story his family used to tell around campfires and other eerie times, just to set the mood. Anderson's grandfather helped construct the vast network of fire towers built between 1934 and the 1960s. After the big fire of 1910, the one that burned most of North Idaho, it was determined that these fire towers were needed to keep a watch and provide an early warning for the forest service, so they could combat the fires more effectively and cut down on the out-of-control burns like the 1910 fire. These towers were built in rugged, untouched wilderness and required a special type of person to build them — woodsmen savvy in construction techniques and horse handling; and not excitable, as they would spend months alone on location constructing these towers. Some of the more difficult locations had two men, but most were done by one. Max Anderson, Mark's grandfather, was one of those men — a true mountain man in every sense.

In May of 1956, Max was assigned to construct a fire tower on Scotchman's Peak, a 6,800-foot peak just outside Clark Fork, Idaho. It was rugged, steep, and, at the time, untouched by man. Anderson would follow game trails to the peak. This was a slow process, as he was driving a team of horses that pulled his camper, a tin-sided shell on wheels. Another, smaller team tied to the back of Anderson's camper pulled a supply cart with building materials that he would need to brace the tower he would construct from trees felled on site.

No chainsaws — just handsaws for felling. Most of the supplies were steel bracing and nails, bolts, nuts, and tar for sealing. Another team of two would come in months later to install windows and finish the interior.

On the fourth night on Scotsman's Peak, Anderson was just settling in for a dinner of squirrel stew and biscuits when he heard the horses. They were upset at something and making a tremendous racket whinnying, kicking, and snorting. Assuming it was a grizzly, Anderson grabbed his .45 Colt revolver and lantern and opened the camper door. What he saw was not a grizzly. He later described seeing a creature approximately eight feet tall, muscular, and covered in hair from head to toe. It was standing in front of the horse corral and just looking at the horses.

When Anderson shined his lantern on the creature, it let out a roar or yell that rocked him to his very soul. It was like nothing he had ever heard in those mountains; nor had he ever seen anything like what he was looking at. He turned to grab his bolt-action Savage 300 for extra firepower. That's when the first boulder struck the camper. It hit with such force that it knocked Anderson to his knees. The boulder had to weigh close to 200 pounds, and this creature just threw it like a ball.

Before Anderson could get to his feet, another boulder hit, then another, and another. Anderson shut the door and lay down on the floor, preparing for the creature to attack. He chambered a round and waited. The boulder stack went on for about fifteen minutes, and then nothing. He waited for almost an hour before daring to open the camper door. The camp was pretty much intact. The horses were still in the corral and were calming down, although they kept focused on the west, as if whatever had been there was still out there. The camper damage was extensive, and there were no less than fifteen boulders scattered around the camper. All of them were 100- to 200-pounders. The forest service had given him a camera to document the work on the tower and other points of interest. At first light, Anderson took several pictures of the camper and the boulders. No one would have believed him otherwise.

There was no salvaging the camper, so Anderson cannibalized it into a small walled structure to sleep in the rest of his time there. He never saw that creature again, even though he was there for four more months. But he did say he always felt as if something was watching him and on occasion heard strange howls echoing throughout the mountains.

The Anderson family still had the photos Max took, and according to Mark, there was no way to fake them. Max swore the story was true, right up until his death in 1985.

"I wonder if this is the same thing," said Mark. "I know we're a long way from Scotsman's, but damn, it kinda sounds like the same thing."

"C'mon, Anderson. Monsters in the woods? Get real!" Pitts wasn't convinced. "These things always prove to be hoaxes, or a man in a monkey suit."

"Well, all I know is my grandpa had the pictures of the damage, and Slim got hurt by something. And what the hell happened to Moore? I mean, even a grizzly, and there are no grizzlies on Hoodoo, would've left more evidence and wouldn't have dragged Moore that far from where it grabbed him. Something's out there."

The other fire teams had heard the chatter on the radios. They didn't know exactly what was happening, but they knew it wasn't good. For sure, at the least, Moore was missing, and something was stalking them, something they were not prepared for. Captain Robertson had radioed the Bonner County Sheriff's Department and notified them of their situation, but there would be no law enforcement presence until the fire was contained. The fire crews were on their own.

Down on the spur road, Nancy Mills and her team were making good progress on widening the fire break, but they weren't 100% focused on the job at hand. Nancy knew that if she didn't get a handle on this, someone else was going to get hurt. And, to top it off, the wind was changing directions and getting stronger. It wasn't just smoke swirling about, but ash and some embers were starting to mix in. This was what they were trying to get ahead of. Embers floating about meant it wouldn't be long before fires would be popping up everywhere.

Below Nancy and her team, Ben Proctor and his team were watching the same thing. Only they were much closer to the fire, and it was getting hot. Everyone worked in two-man teams with the team leaders eyeing the forest for anything out of the ordinary. A tough job, given the circumstances — night, smoke, fire, wind, rugged terrain, and someone or something out there that seemed to have a grudge against them.

Nancy got on the radio to Ben. "Hey, Sqautch, the wind's really picking up. What's it looking like where you are?" She really just wanted to hear Ben's voice. It calmed her nerves.

"Degrading fast, Nancy. We're nowhere near ready for back-burns yet. How goes it with you guys? You okay with all the shit going on?" Ben was trying not to sound overly worried, but he always felt a bit anxious when Nancy was in harm's way.

"We're good, but a little on edge. Slim looked pretty bad, and they saw something back down the road. Now, I think Moore's disappeared, and from what I could hear, it's ugly-bad. I've got the team shotgun, and I'm watching as close as I can, but visibility sucks."

"I'm with you, Nance. We're doing the same. Be careful!"

Nancy could tell by Ben's voice, he was more concerned than usual, and that gave her that warm feeling. She didn't dwell on that for long. After all, she wasn't some teenage girl with a high school crush. She was a fire team leader, and she needed to focus on her team and the task in front of her.

As the creature moved through the cave, it sensed a change in its environment. The one threat to its land it couldn't do anything about — the fire — was starting to move. The cave system had been used by its kind ever since they came to this mountain. It had two natural entrances; one on the west, one on the east. There were two other cave entrances, which were created by the creature's ancestors as a way to navigate the lands without being seen. The openings were well hidden on the northern and southern faces. The cross breezes formed by this configuration helped keep the cave vented. This meant that the smoke from the fire would clear fairly quickly if it did get in. If it needed to, the creature could stay in the cave for days, or until the fire passed. That is, if it had food.

Most of the larger food sources had fled the mountain because of the fire, and it would too if it were to find enough food for its group. It had ventured down to the valley before, but it was risky. There were food sources it knew it could gather quickly and then return to the mountain. It would have to be fast, as the enemy was already at hand, and the fire was closing in. As it approached the southern opening, it sniffed the air for any scent of danger. It moved slowly to the entrance and paused to make sure the route was clear. It would be reaching the valley in the early morning — not the best time to forage, but it had no choice. As it neared the flatlands below Hoodoo Mountain, it could hear the noises it knew meant danger. People. But more importantly, it could smell food. What it was smelling were the goats and chickens that Randy Scott kept in pens that were set up along the forest edge. It had been there before, when it was much younger, but it was dark then, and there were few dangers between the food and its lands. It would have to take a different approach if it was to remain unseen.

It didn't know that, not too many years earlier, people had moved into what it thought was untouched forest. As it got closer to the area, it smelled both familiar and unexpected aromas, and it froze as it saw movement to its left. The dog had alerted the human to its presence, and instinct took over. Survival instinct. Its mission was food for the group and to return to protect its lands. Nothing more. As noted earlier, it had an intelligence about it. It could reason and choose between pure reaction and necessity. It would have to take a different trail to the food.

5

THE SIGHTING, JULY 6

Chuck Brewer was working as a route delivery driver for Schwan's Food Service. His route took him into some of the most remote and rugged territories of Northern Idaho. His route required him to spend four nights a week away from home, leaving his wife, Jean, alone to manage their five-acre property. Jean was used to doing everything necessary to keep the home and property cared for. Her ex-husband barely lifted a finger around the house. His main accomplishment was abandoning the family. After that, Jean did everything from caring for three children and five grandchildren to changing the oil in the vehicles, along with all their other equipment maintenance. She was used to living somewhat isolated, as she and her family used to live at the top of a mountain in western Washington state. There were mountain lions, bears, bobcats, and a variety of other critters around her on that mountain. Not much scared her.

Her and Chuck met on one of those online dating services and hit it off right away. With Jean's children grown and on their own, she moved to Sprit Lake, Idaho with Chuck to start a fresh life.

Every morning, Jean would get up and do her walk around the property. They had cut a trail that looped through the woods and connected to their gravel drive. Seven times around was a mile, which Jean did almost daily. Today's walk would prove a bit more eventful.

The first thing Jean noticed when she stepped out on the porch was the smoke. It was bad. Most days this summer had been smokey, but this seemed thick. The last fire report she looked at showed the closest fires were over thirty miles away. She knew this smoke was from a fire that had to be much closer than that. There was ash falling out of this smoke. Although walking and breathing in the smoke was unpleasant, it would not deter her from her walk.

"C'mon, Sampson! Let's go for a walk." Sampson was their German shepherd mix, and he loved walking the trail. He was a sweet dog; not a mean bone in his body.

The walk had barely begun when Sampson crouched low, turned towards the open field next to the property line, and started to growl. This was a deep, throaty growl. A threatening growl. Sampson's hair rose, and he froze. Jean was taken aback. Sampson had never growled at anything as long as she had had him, let alone a growl that would send any attacker running in fear of being eaten.

"What's the matter, boy? What'd you see, huh?" Jean looked over to where Sampson was staring and immediately froze with fear.

Chuck was driving his truck from the hotel in Clark Fork, Idaho and heading to start his route in Hope, just a few miles down the road. His cell phone rang, and he saw it was Jean. He always worried something bad would happen while he was working so far out of town, and Jean never called unless it was important.

Chuck picked up the phone. "What's up, honey? Everything okay?"

"I'm not sure," Jean said with a quiver in her voice. "I just saw something, and I don't know what it was."

She told Chuck about Sampson's growling and how that shocked her. Chuck was confused at that, too. Chuck had had that dog for ten years, and never once had he growled at anything.

Jean continued her account of the sighting.

"So, I turn to look where Sampson is staring, and I see this, this *thing*. At first, I thought it was a man, but he would've been a huge man. That grass in the field is four feet tall, and this thing was at least four or five feet taller than that. Then I noticed it was covered with hair. *White* hair. I can only describe it as like a polar bear. It was looking right at me, and I could see it was *not* a bear. Its face was flat like a person's but covered with this hair. I had my cell phone with me, so I went to take a picture, and the damn battery was dead. Just when I lifted up my phone, this thing yelled at me. Not in a human tone — more like some kind of beast. It was blood curdling. I've never heard anything like it before. I thought it was going to charge me. Hell, it was only forty-five or so yards away. I started to step backwards, and that's when this thing took off running. Not on four legs, but *two*. I watched it until it disappeared into the woods across the road. And you know that fence along the road? It didn't jump it. It just sort of stepped over it on a full-out run. I figure it ran seventy-five yards in the time it took me to take three steps back. What the hell did I just see, Chuck?"

Chuck couldn't believe it, but Jean wasn't prone to exaggerations or tall tales.

"Sounds like a damn white bigfoot. Holy shit! You just saw a damn bigfoot. I'm a long way away. Let me call Pete and see if he's home. Stay inside, and I'll call you right back.

Pete Wilson was Chuck and Jean's neighbor to the east. They shared a fence along the gravel drive. Maybe Pete could check things out.

Chuck got a hold of Pete, but he was out at a job site. Chuck knew he was probably going to get teased when he told Pete there might be a bigfoot in the neighborhood, and a white one at that. But, when Chuck finished relaying the story, instead of teasing, there was silence for a few seconds, and then Pete said, "You know, this morning, when I went to let the dogs out, they wouldn't go out. I had to force them out the door, and then they wouldn't leave the damn porch. I left them out there for almost twenty minutes, and they never left the porch. When I opened the door, all three of them high-tailed it in and all hid under stuff — the table, the bed. Their damn tails were tucked. Something scared them. I also noticed my horses acting up.

They were whinnying and bucking, and they were up here by the house. They are always at the fence by your drive. Something was out there. I figured a bear, but not a damn sasquatch. Holy shit, Chuck!"

Now Chuck was worried. He wouldn't be home until well after dark. He was going to ask Pete to check things out when he got home, but Pete was ahead of him on that.

"If you want, I'll check things out when I go home, and I'll give you a call and let you know what I find."

"I appreciate it, Pete." Chuck felt much better. Pete was a retired Marine and an avid hunter. If anyone would know what to look for, it was Pete.

"Hey, honey." Chuck was relieved Jean answered her cell phone on the first ring. "I spoke with Pete and he's going to take a look around when he gets home. Do me a favor and stay inside as much as you can today, will you?"

Jean usually hated being cooped up in the house but agreed to Chuck's request.

"No problem, baby. Sampson's lying on the floor, and he's not looking right. It's like he's scared or something. That's got me freaked out a little. Besides, the smoke's really bad. I think there's a fire close by, and there's a nasty smell in the air too. Smells like burnt death."

The day couldn't go by any slower for Chuck. He kept looking at his phone, anticipating Pete's call. It finally came at 7:30 that night.

"You ain't gonna believe this" were the first words out of Pete's mouth. "First, the ground's so fuckin' hard from how dry it's been that there are no footprints to be found. If Jean had seen a moose or large deer, it would have left some marks in the dirt, even when it's this hard. Nothin'. There is what looks like could be a footprint in the gravel road. It's a huge indentation in the gravel. Maybe sixteen inches. Then there's nothing for about six feet, and then there's another indentation about sixteen inches long. If that's what she saw, it's running on two legs, and six feet is a pretty large stride."

Chuck was listening intently, imagining everything Pete was describing. It was all at once exciting and scary. Exciting that something as elusive as Bigfoot could be lurking in the woods surrounding their home. Scary, because what would a creature like this be capable of?

"There's something else." Pete's deadpan voice sounded chilling. "You know that four-foot-high fence along the property line?"

"Yeah," said Chuck.

"Well, it's laid flat on the ground right where Jean said this thing went. The metal post is bent flat to the ground like something just pushed it over with its foot or something. I've never seen anything like it before. I'm not saying what it is. I'm just sayin' I've never seen anything like this before."

"Thanks, Pete. I'll be home about ten tonight. I really appreciate you doing that. Man, I hate being so far away when all the good shit happens."

"Anytime, Chuck. By the way, there's a fire up in Blanchard up by Hoodoo Mountain. That's only a few miles from here, so stay on your toes."

"Holy shit! That *is* close. Too close. Will do, buddy. I'll talk to you this weekend."

It was no wonder the smoke was so bad. That fire was almost right down the street. They would have to be vigilant and be prepared for anything — including white, hairy beasts. Chuck couldn't help but wonder if the fire and the drought had any connection to this sighting. He wanted so much to see it for himself. He had always been a Bigfoot devotee and even thought of doing a search for the legendary cryptid. He couldn't help but be a little jealous of Jean for seeing a possible bigfoot. *Lucky stiff.*

Heading down the dark, wooded, private road to his drive. Chuck peered through every shadow hoping to see a glimpse of the white beast, but the woods were quiet and still. He noticed a slight odor in the air as he turned down his gravel drive.

Man, that stinks, he thought. *What made that hideous smell?*

Chuck was greeted at the door by Jean, but Sampson was nowhere to be seen.

"Where's my good dog, huh? Where's my Sampson?"

"He's been in the bedroom all day. Won't leave unless I call him."
Jean's face had just a touch of fear on it. "It's kinda freaking me out."

Later the next day, Chuck did his own scouting of the area. He
saw the prints in the gravel, he saw the bent-over fence, and he found
something else. It wasn't much, but it was something interesting.
Being an avid hunter, Chuck loved finding and identifying tracks.
Chuck got down on his hands and knees and examined the area
where Jean said the creature had stood. He found a tuft of grass that
was smashed down, and in the dirt, he found a smudge that
measured seventeen inches long. If this was a hoofed animal, the
smudge would have had crisp edges, not soft ones. And he didn't
know of any hoofed animal that had a seventeen-inch hoof. There
was a second smudge in the same direction the beast ran, but that
was it. Nothing more for tracks. No hair, no definable prints, no
evidence that could be used to identify what Jean saw.

Later that night, Chuck searched "white bigfoot" on YouTube and
came up with a video taken in Pennsylvania. The video was clear and
showed what looked to be a white bigfoot. But the interesting thing in
the video was when the creature yelled at the person filming.

Chuck called Jean into the room. "Close your eyes. I want you to
listen to something." Chuck had not told her he was looking up
Bigfoot stuff or what she was going to listen for. "Now, tell me what
you think." He had paused the video just before the yell. When he hit
play and the creature on the film made its noise, Jean said, "That's it.
That's what that thing did. That's what it's yell sounded like, only
much louder."

Chuck could tell Jean was a little shaken from hearing that yell
again. It wouldn't be the last time they would hear that scream.

Chuck became slightly obsessed with researching the creature.
He found numerous articles referencing the "Hoodoo Howler." It
was, as of yet, unattributed to any known animal. Chuck had a pretty
good idea what the "Howler" was.

"You know what? I'm gonna hang a couple of my game cameras
out along the fence line and over by that game trail on the back side
of the property. Might get lucky."

After the encounter with the human, it circled back through the undeveloped state land along Clagstone Road and made its way to the bounty it was seeking. Goats. They were easy prey and would provide enough food to last until the fire passed. As it approached the fence line that bordered the state land, it paused and scanned the goat enclosure for the biggest, fattest, ones. It knew it could carry four goats without much problem. It also studied the area for any signs of danger. All was quiet, so it moved in slowly towards the pens, using any cover available to conceal its movements.

Once the prey animals were selected, it moved quickly over the fence and snapped the necks of the four fattest goats. It gathered them up under its massive arms and started back to its lands and the fight ahead. But, before leaving the bounty of easy pickings, it feasted on chicken eggs, shell and all, and one chicken from the nearby coop, leaving the goats for the group. It was a smokey morning, making it a bit easier to stay hidden while it moved across gravel back roads and forested tracts of state land before finally reaching the southern base of Hoodoo Mountain. It would make its way to the southern entrance to its lair, delivering the meal of fresh-killed goat to the group. They would stay in the cave most of the day to rest. Moving about during the day with so many humans on the mountain would be dangerous, even with the heavy smoke offering cover for their movements. They would wait for night and the cover of limited visibility.

6

DISCOVERY, JULY 7

The fire was making a drastic move around the mountain. Northeasterly winds blowing steadily at fifteen miles per hour with gusts to thirty-five pushed the fire quickly around the southern and western faces, threatening to cut off the firefighters from the escape route to the south. The northern escape route meant going uphill and over sixteen miles of rough, old, overgrown logging roads. Fire moves fastest uphill, so keeping the fire contained would be crucial to maintaining evacuation routes.

Ben "Squatch" Proctor got on the radio to Nancy. The fire was pushing dangerously close to his team, and he knew they would have to relocate and possibly join another team to double the efforts to widen fire breaks up higher if they were to get the foothold they wanted.

"Hey, Nance, we're gonna move up to your north side and help with the fire break. If we get a backfire going, we might be able to stop the fire from spreading up the west face. You heard from the captain yet?"

Nancy was more than a little happy to hear Ben was coming up to them. "No word yet, Ben. I think he was grabbing Toothless and his guys and taking them over to Stumpy's location. I'll try to raise him on the horn."

Captain Roberson and Toothless were delayed by a tree that came down right in front of their truck. Pitts and Anderson saw it come down, but Robertson signaled for them to keep going. They were to rendezvous with Stumpy's team and help with the fire break until Robertson got there.

"Holy shit! Holy fuckin' shit! This damn mountain is tryin' to kill us, Cap." Toothless was understandably freaked out by everything that had happened in the last few hours.

Robertson was a little shaken himself by the tree coming down so close to the truck. But he wasn't about to let Toothless see it.

"Calm down, Toothless. Trees come down all the time in these mountains. Winds are gusting pretty good, and it's probably not the last one we'll see." He knew they didn't normally fall in front of them, though.

"Grab a chainsaw, and let's get this done fast."

"Cap, this is Mills. Come in, Cap!"

"Go, Mills. Robertson here."

"Squatch's team is getting ready to move to our location. Fire's moving in on his team, and we need to finish this fire break so we can start our backfire. Ten-four?"

"Ten-four, Mills. Me and Toothless are blocked by a down tree, but we're working on it. Pitts and Anderson are heading to Stumpy. Hold your ground, and when we get free from this, we'll make our way to you and see if we can start that backfire. Robertson out."

"Ten-four, Cap. Squatch, you copy that?"

"Roger that, Nance. See you soon."

Pitts and Anderson made it to Stumpy and Team B's location. Stumpy wanted the scoop on the situation with Jesse Moore and Toothless. "What's goin' on, guys? What happened to Moore?"

Pitts tried to give Stumpy the best answer he could, but he wasn't completely sure what was going on. "All we know, Stump, is Moore's probably dead. Toothless said something grabbed him and dragged him up the mountain. Said he saw a print of some kind of monster or somethin', and blood, lots of blood, but no body."

Stumpy just stared at Pitts for a few seconds with that what-the-fuck-are-you-talking-about? look.

"Are you tellin' me Moore was killed by a monster? What kind of crap is that?"

"Pitts is right, Stumpy. Toothless is pretty shook up, and that *never* happens. Kinda got us a little nervous, too. I mean, what could be doin' all this shit? First Slim, then Moore. What next?"

"I'm sure there's a more reasonable explanation for all this besides monsters. Holy shit! Get a grip, guys!" Even Stumpy felt an uneasiness over the events that had transpired during the night. But monsters? He just couldn't wrap his head around that one.

At about that time, Stumpy's radio crackled to life. It was Ben Proctor.

"Stumpy? This is Squatch. You copy?"

"Go, Squatch. We read ya'."

"Get your team rounded up and head up to Mills' southern flank. We need to get that fire break widened and start the backfire as soon as possible. This fire's moving fast, and we're gonna get overrun if we don't move."

"Roger, that, Squatch. Watch you don't get your ass burned on your way out."

"Worry about your own stubby ass." There was a bit of levity to try and diffuse everyone's tension.

Captain Robertson and Toothless were just finishing clearing the fallen tree that had them blocked from the rest of the crew.

"Well, Cap, that didn't take too long."

"Good deal, Toothless. Let's get the hell down the mountain."

Toothless had never moved as fast in his life as he did while cutting up that fallen tree. He could only think that whatever killed Moore was still up here with them.

"Cap, what the hell is on this damn mountain?" Toothless was noticeably scared.

"Not sure, Welch. Never heard of or seen anything like this

before." Robertson couldn't help but think about those words Jimmy Two Horns had said to him when they got to the mountain.

"Four trucks in, two trucks out. Death on the mountain." They were already down one truck, and for sure one firefighter was missing, probably dead. Was there something to this legend of Seatco? Was there something on this mountain other than the fire he and his team needed to fight? He found his mind starting to wander as he pondered Jimmy's words and the events of the past few hours. The radio crackling to life snapped him out of his fog.

"Proctor to Captain Robertson. Come in!"

Robertson picked up the radio. "Go ahead, Ben. What you got?"

"Teams A and B have moved to Team C's twenty."

Twenty was code for location and a standard for all first responders.

We have spread out on that firebreak and should be ready for that backfire in a couple hours. Fire's moving fast around the base and starting to move up."

"Ten-four, Ben. We're almost to ya'."

The three teams were now separated by over two miles along the firebreak, with Team A along the south, Team B on the north end, and Team C somewhere in the middle. B and A teams were focused on lengthening and turning the firebreak down the mountain to try and surround the fire and snuff it out with the backfire before it gathered momentum and sped past the fire lines. Nancy Mills and her team were working to connect the fire breaks that the other teams were creating so there would be one continuous fire break to light the back-burn from. The going was tough, as the smoke from the fire below was funneling straight up the two natural drainages that were on either end of the fire break.

A drainage was just what it sounded like. They were creases in the natural landscape created by snow and rain runoff down the mountain. Erosion from this formed those creases and they usually drained into creeks or rivers. Some spilled into fissures in the rocks and would run underground either into the aquifer or subterranean creeks. Drainages made good corridors for game animals to traverse the terrain due to the cover provided by the natural depression in the earth.

Wind currents generally flowed down in the morning and up at night. Any predators lying in wait or stalking them could easily be smelled out due to these usually predictable air flows. Fires, on the other hand, created their own air flows, disrupting normal daily animal migrations between food sources and bedding areas. Predators used drainages to ambush prey, lying in wait just off of the drainage so their scent would, hopefully, not flow directly into the drainage. Mother Nature's game of chess.

Chess... That was one way to describe the events that would unfold on Hoodoo Mountain over the next few days. A life-and-death game of chess.

Robertson and Toothless reached Mills' location about sunrise — best anyone could tell because of the smoke.

"Mills, take Toothless here and scavenge whatever you can from that busted truck. We're gonna need all the gear we can get on this one. And, Mills... don't forget the extra shotgun shells."

Robertson paused and stared at Nancy with a look that froze her. He didn't have to say the words, but the message was conveyed to her perfectly. His look said "we're in for the fight of our lives." And not just from the fire.

"Roger, Cap."

Mills and Toothless stripped the truck of everything usable that the teams could carry — food, gear, extra canteens, and, yes, the extra shotgun shells. They loaded everything onto two field stretchers and latched it all down as best as they could to minimize the chance of spilling vital gear and rations in case they needed to cover ground fast. Everything went on the stretchers except the shotgun shells. Those went into Nancy's pack. She wasn't taking any chances on losing them on this mountain. She might not have believed in monsters, but something was on this mountain, and the evidence pointed to either a crazed psycho or something else. Either way, she had the shotgun, and that gave her some semblance of control.

Captain Robertson radioed the other team captains and

instructed them to retrieve the extra shotgun shells from their trucks as well. He wasn't convinced there was a monster hunting his crews, but he wasn't taking any chances either. For all he knew, there was a psycho up there with them, and he was going to make sure his people were protected.

It had been over two hours without any attacks, and the crews were working feverishly to complete the fire breaks. There were four teams of two felling trees to keep them from falling across the fire breaks. If a tree were to fall across the fire break, it could act as a bridge for fire to cross the break and move the fire uphill. So the trees were dropped so they would fall downhill, effectively destroying any bridges along the breaks. It was quite a sight to see as tree after tree fell in the same direction in a dangerous dance between trees weighing tons and the tiny human "beavers" felling them.

All the while there was the buzzing of the saws, the billowing smoke, and the ever-increasing ash and ember showers. All the while, there were the fervent movements of the crews clearing brush and debris, their shadows distorted by the ever-flowing smoke, looking like ghosts moving through the forest while sentinels stood guard with their shotguns, scanning the forest for anything posing a threat to their teams, their friends, their surrogate family. Any one of them would have given their life for the other if need be.

That is the epitome of love. The Bible states that there is no love greater than for one person to give his life for another, and these fire-fighters would do just that. Some may be asked to do just that while on this mountain.

"Hey, Stumpy, get over here *quick!*" Craig Stephens and Bruce Dutchauser had been working the far end of the northern section of the fire break when they discovered a gruesome sight.

"What's up, Stephens? What ya' need?" Stumpy hated running through the woods unnecessarily. He was, after all, carrying a few extra pounds on slightly shorter legs than most of the crew.

"Sam, you need to get over here and see this for yourself." There it was again. Stephens didn't say Stumpy, he said Sam. No one called him Sam unless it was important.

When Sam got to Stephens and Dutchauser, he saw them standing and looking down at something on the ground.

"What's up, guys? Did you find gold or somethin' up here?"

Stephens never looked up. He just pointed down and said, "Not exactly, Sam. Look."

Sam looked down to see a blood-soaked wallet and some bloody, shredded clothing. There was some unidentifiable remnants of flesh in the mix and what looked like a vertebrae.

"What the fuck? Where's the rest of the body? Any signs nearby, guys?"

Sam was stunned. In all his years of fighting fires in the wilderness, he had never seen anything like this. Dead deer? Yes. Dead moose? Yes. Shredded human remains? No. Sam bent down to retrieve the wallet. Maybe there would be something in there to identify the victim. He carefully opened it and found a driver's license.

"Brandon Rucker." It's one thing to see a dead body, severed limbs, or eviscerated entrails when they are not associated with anyone. It's another thing completely when those remains have a name.

"Geez, Sam. What the fuck did that?" Dutchauser was almost shaking from the adrenaline from the sudden fear that struck him.

"Don't know, Dutch. Probably a hunter or hiker got hurt or died up here, and the critters found him. I wouldn't read too much into this."

Sam was not so sure though. Too much of a coincidence to find these remains in the same general area in light of recent events. And the remains were only a day or two old, best as he could figure.

"Better get a ziplock from the truck and bag what's here. The sheriff's gonna want them. I'll take a quick look around to see if there's any other remains in the area."

Stephens ran back to the trucks to get the plastic bag. When he looked at the bag, it hit him. What was left of someone's body would fit neatly into a small plastic bag. He didn't know the victim, but it brought him to tears. By the looks of the driver's license, the victim wasn't very old. That always seemed to hit first responders the hardest. So young to die, especially to be torn apart the way he was.

When Stumpy got the remains packed up and back to the team's trucks, he got Captain Robertson to radio the find in to the Bonner County sheriff's office along with the GPS location of where they were found. Even if the fire overran other remains, they would know where to start looking. Maybe they could locate lager remains for the family. No family should have to bury a cigar box-sized casket with virtually no remains inside. The Sheriff's office would not respond until the scene was secured and safe, so collecting whatever they could from the scene and pinpointing the location with GPS was paramount.

"Get that bag packed in a cooler, Stump, and make sure it's double-bagged. Don't want any leaks in there."

As Stumpy started for the truck, he heard a loud, almost sorrowful, growling sound, coupled with the sound of breaking branches and heavy footfalls. Something was coming his way and fast. And it sounded huge. He only had time to turn to face what was coming and brace. Just a few seconds after he heard it coming, it broke free from the underbrush just ten or fifteen yards away. It was a bear. A huge grizzly bear. Stumpy thought he was about to meet his end, but the bear just kept running away from the fire. That's when Stumpy saw that the bear was wounded. There was a large wood splinter protruding from the bear's right side. It was almost as if someone had speared it.

Stumpy knew right away what had probably happened. A lot of times during forest fires, trees explode from the high heat. Most of the trees in the northwest are pine or fir trees. These trees are full of sap or resin, which is highly flammable. When one of these trees becomes super-heated by fire, the resins can boil and expand violently, resulting in an explosion. These exploding trees blast wooden splinters in all directions and hundreds of feet away. Some of these splinters are as long as six feet and can be deadly. It's one of the hazards fire crews are always on the watch for. This poor bear was in the wrong place at the wrong time and was too close to one of these exploding trees. Stumpy watched as the bear stumbled up the mountain and eventually succumbed to its injury.

"Poor bastard." That's all that could be said, and as Stumpy turned back to put the baggie in the cooler, he said the same words about Brandon Rucker.

The fire was reaching an area damaged by pine beetles. A large swath of trees had been killed by the beetle locals called "stump fuckers."

The invasive pine beetle has plagued the north Idaho forests, decimating hundreds of acres throughout the area. Once a tree is attacked by the beetle, it is done for. Trees die from the top down, and their carnage can be seen from far away. Most of the damaged trees are cut down by firewood collectors for use in their wood stoves, but many are either unreachable or in terrain that would add more work to the retrieval than it's worth. The state has battled the beetle with various tactics, from harvesting the wood via logging operations and firewood permits to the public, to even introducing a natural predator, the yellow jacket, into the area.

The little yellow stingers feed on the beetle's larvae and can drastically cut down on the beetle population if the method works. One million queens were released into the forest to try and quell the invasion. That didn't work very well. In fact, the only thing that seemed to accomplish was to create the worst summer of yellow jacket swarms and a huge increase in people being stung by the little black and yellow insects.

Ironically, burning the infested trees is the most effective way to eradicate the beetles, and fire was getting close to eliminating about 50,000 of them from Hoodoo Mountain.

A fire in that tract of timber would be like pouring gasoline on it, causing an inferno so large, it would quickly overrun any efforts put forth by Robertson's teams. They had no way of knowing the fire's embers were starting to float towards the tinder-dry dead-standing trees. Once the fire reached those trees, its flames would wick up into the canopy, creating what's known to firefighters as a candle. It's when a standing tree catches fire and burns from the top down, resembling a candle, and it is a very dangerous event. Not only can the whole top of the tree collapse to the ground, causing an explosion of flying, burning shrapnel and embers; but also, trees can actually explode, sending flaming debris across vast areas and igniting areas far beyond the main fire. This is how many fires cover so much ground in such short time. It was a race against time, and time was running out.

"Mills, Squatch, and Stumpy, light 'em up!" Robertson was giving the order for the teams to start the backfires. Hopefully, it wasn't too late; the winds were picking up and coming in more from the west, straight up the mountain. If the backfires didn't burn enough of the fuel before the main fire reached the lower fire breaks, the fire would most likely overrun the upper fire break and move towards the crest.

Starting the backfires was always a precarious dance. If a gust blew before the backfire took hold, the fire could jump the line and cross into the timber above the fire teams, trapping them between two fires with little room for evading the flames and intense heat. What they hoped to see was the backfires leaning towards the main fire. That would indicate the main fire was sucking air into itself, providing the all-important oxygen it needed to continue to grow and consume more and more fuel. In fact, the back-burns would starve the fire of the very fuel it needed to grow and eventually weaken it to where the firefighters could get the upper hand. A delicate dance, indeed.

Then, as if it had been waiting for the teams to commit to the back-burns, the wind picked up, and the embers swarmed in like glowing orange clouds covering the firefighting teams and migrating up the mountain. The firefighters all braced against the onslaught of hot embers exploding all around them. A sudden gust blew burning embers past the crews and up the mountain.

"Shit!" Robertson knew the winds would likely negate the back-burn efforts. "Get your gear, and let's move the trucks out of here before we get pinned between two fire fronts. Rally at the helipad! At least from there we can cross over the top if we need to."

Robertson didn't have to say it twice. Everyone moved quickly to gather equipment and load it into the trucks. The team leaders rounded up their people and made sure everyone was safely in the trucks before they got in. Once everyone was set, the caravan of trucks sped up the spur road up the mountain towards the helipad — the same spur road Robertson, Welch, Pitts, and Anderson had come down just a couple of hours earlier. They couldn't help but feel they were heading back into serious danger from something other than the fire. Even those who weren't eyewitnesses to the events involving Jesse Moore felt icy fear and trepidation flowing through their veins.

Jackson Matoskah was silent. He wasn't chatty. Matoskah subscribed to the philosophy of "talk low, talk slow, and don't say very much." But even for him, he was quiet now. Like everyone else, he had heard the radio chatter as the events of the night unfolded. Just like everyone else, he was scared. But unlike everyone else, Jack felt there was something he was missing. Something in the stories told to him by his grandfather and father. Something about what was happening up on the mountain. He had been so young when the stories of the Seatco and the lost tribe were told. Still, there was something eating at him about those stories. Was there something he knew that could help his teammates? Then, there was the strange feeling he got when Jimmy Two Horns seemed to look right into his soul, like Jimmy knew he would be the key. But what was it?

"Hey, Jack, why so quiet?" Dave Wilson could see Jack was lost in thought. "Don't worry, bud. We'll get outta this. We got our own sasquatch."

Jackson managed a weak grin. "Yeah, and Proctor's starting to smell like a squatch, too."

Everyone in the truck got a laugh at that, and for a moment, all seemed normal — as normal as things could be while racing up a ragged spur road trying to outrun a raging forest fire at the same time something besides the fire was trying to kill everyone. Perfectly normal situation.

Jackson's thoughts took over, and, once again, he got that faraway, glazed stare one does as they try to picture events from the past. If only he could remember what it was about those damn stories.

Everyone was staring out at the tree lines, looking for anything out of the ordinary. It was a surreal sight as the trucks bounded up the spur road, fire crews rocking with every bump and rut. All the while, team leaders literally rode shotgun.

The sun was streaming through the smoke and looking like smokey rays piercing the landscape all around the helipad site. It looked magical and spooky at the same time. The trucks pulled into the helipad and were positioned for a quick getaway if need be.

"Hey, Mills, get some eyes up on that staging platform so we can keep an eye on that fire line." Captain Robertson knew her crew had the youngest climbing legs and keenest eyes of all the firefighters there.

"On it, Cap. Wilson, take Spud and get up there. And here, take this shotgun with you. Just in case. But don't forget where you got it, Dave."

Take the shotgun? That just brought everything back to reality. They were at the site of Moore's disappearance and were going to scramble up a hundred yards of scrub brush and loose rocks, right through where signs of his struggle and ultimate demise were, then up to the area a logging company carved out a staging area for the equipment used to haul timber from below and up to the helipad for removal. It was on an exposed cliff face and had excellent views of the landscape below. Even with the smoke, they should be able to see where the fire line was, how fast it was moving, and in which direction.

"Last one to the top buys the first round of beer." Wilson had the advantage, as he was used to moving quickly while carrying a thirty-six-inch chainsaw. This time, his chainsaw was at the truck, and Frye (Spud) was carrying the shotgun.

"You're on, but I get a twenty-yard head start.

"Go!" Wilson only gave him ten yards. After all, he wanted that first free beer.

The two sprinted up towards the staging area, deftly hopping over rocks and dead-falls almost without effort. Youth and conditioning were a great edge to have. Spud was maintaining a slight space between the two, but Wilson was closing, until Spud stopped suddenly. Wilson started to blow past him, but Spud grabbed him.

"Hey! That's cheating, Spud. What the hell's wrong with you?"

Spud pointed up the ridge just to their right. There, just below the staging area, was a tree. Nothing extraordinary about this tree, except it was standing. Upside down. This wasn't a small tree, either. The tree was probably about a thousand pounds and definitely placed in that position. The root ball was at the top, giving the tree a strange kind of canopy.

"Holy shit! What the hell is that?"

Wilson and Spud looked at the strange tree for a minute, then their radios crackled to life.

"What the hell's going on up there? You guys okay?" Mills had been watching the two's progress and saw them stop. Her first thought was that one of them got hurt or something.

"We're good, Nance. But there's something weird up here. We're gonna check it out real quick."

"What is it?"

"A tree. But it's planted upside down. And it ain't no tiny tree either."

Nancy knew Wilson wasn't the type to jump to conclusions or go off the deep end on things, so she figured it was something that needed to be looked at a little closer.

Jackson Matoskah heard the transmission too. There was something about upside-down trees in one of his grandfather's stories. He felt an overwhelming need to see the tree.

"Nancy, I would like to take a look at that tree, if I can." He almost didn't wait for her response to head up.

"Why, Jack? It's probably just the timber crew's idea of a practical joke. It's pretty close to where their staging equipment was, and it wouldn't be a problem for them to put a tree in the ground upside down."

"Maybe, but I would still like to take a look."

The tone in Jackson's voice convinced Nancy to let him go.

"Okay, Jack. But don't take too much time. We got a fire to babysit.

Send one of those other guys to the staging area so we can keep an eye on our job."

"Will do, boss."

With that, Jackson made his way up the trail towards Wilson and Spud.

"Spud, Mills wants you to head up to the staging area. Wilson and I are going to scope out that tree." Jackson and Wilson were the type of friends who didn't need to say a lot for the other to know what they were thinking. They were both level-headed and had seen a lot of strange things in the woods. But never an upside-down tree.

Spud made his way to the staging area and Winslow and Matoskah headed over to the tree.

"What're you thinkin', Jack? This tree mean something?"

Jackson didn't want to say too much about stories, legends, monsters, or lost tribes. "Just never seen an upside-down tree before."

Wilson knew there was more. He knew Jackson too well. He also knew not to push the issue, so he shrugged it off.

"Me, neither. Could be a joke or something."

As they got closer to the tree, Jackson noticed something that proved the loggers didn't do it.

"What's missing, Dave?"

Wilson looked intensely at the tree but couldn't figure out what Jackson was talking about. "Not sure. What?"

"Well, for one thing, there's no claw marks from the crane grabber on the tree. They would have had to use some piece of heavy equipment to do this. There're no cable scars, no big chunks of bark missing from any type of equipment touching this tree."

Wilson was stunned. There wasn't any type of scarring on the bark. Even if they pushed it up with a tractor or something, it would have scraped bark off the tree.

"Holy shit, Jack. What the hell did this?"

Jackson wanted to tell Wilson everything he thought but wanted to look the tree over a bit more. He wouldn't get the chance. Spud had reached the staging area and was scanning the fire line and noticed it was moving faster than anticipated. Embers had blown back up the mountain and over the backfire lines. It was also spreading sideways along the beetle-damaged timber at an alarming speed. It wouldn't be long before the fire crews would be cut off from any of the traditional escape routes provided by the access roads. On top of that, a huge explosion rocked the mountain from below. It was the broken-down truck's fuel tanks blowing, and it spewed flaming gasoline in every direction.

"Hey, boss." Spud was radioing what he was seeing to Mills. "That fire is about to overrun our backfire line. It's spreading north and south too."

"Well, guys, this fire's gonna test the shit out of us. Fuckin' wind! They'll never let those planes bring in water drops while it's blowing this bad."

Robertson knew he and his crews were on their own for now. His focus was on the fire; for the time being, the other fight on this mountain faded from the forefront.

"Mills, get your guys back down here, now! We gotta move on this fire, and I mean *now*."

"Spud, Jack, Dave, get your asses back down here asap!

Before entering the cave system with its food for the group, it crept around to see what the humans were doing. When they lit the back-burns, it had no way of knowing they were trying to help. It viewed the act as an attack on it and the group's territory.

They had to be stopped before they destroyed everything the group depended on for survival.

It would retreat to the cave system and deliver the food to the group and rest. It would be dark soon enough, and then it would leave the safety of the caves to do what was necessary for the survival of its species. Just like it had done before. Just like its ancestors had done from the beginning.

The group greeted him in order of the hierarchy within the group. First, the alpha female would great him, followed by the oldest to youngest, males first. This ritual served to remind all of the pecking order. Challenges to this hierarchy were rare and usually dealt with quickly by the alpha male. All decisions for the group or tribe were made by the alpha male and carried out without hesitation. Even mating between members of the tribe was only allowed after the alpha male allowed it. It was his duty to keep the tribe small so it could remain hidden. But the tribe also needed to be strong for all to survive, which could only be accomplished through careful breeding. If the tribe became too large, the alpha male would choose one male and two females to leave the tribe to form their own group. These offshoots of the original group would often relocate fifty to a hundred miles away from the original tribe. This was necessary to keep the concentrations of these tribes low so as to keep their presence undiscovered. Each tribe would mark their territory with a series of snapped-over trees placed in an interwoven pattern. To the untrained or uneducated eye, it would simply look like storm damage. Other tribes would "plant" trees upside down in prominent locations that could be seen from some distance. The tops of these trees were snapped off and the root ball would be in the air. As obvious as this may seem, many of these marker trees went unnoticed by those who happened upon them. Whatever the way the tribe chose to mark their boundaries, they all had one thing in common. Each tribe created a distinct marking that would be scratched onto the boundary marking. Some Native Americans believed these markings served to prove that these markers were, in fact, deliberately placed and not an accident of nature. This, in itself could put some fear into those who might find them and thereby further deter anyone considering continuing farther into the tribe's lands.

Even with all the attempts to ward off trespassers, there was a time in the distant history of the tribes where there was limited interaction with humans. These interactions were often initiated by the humans, and done with respect for the tribe's territory, when needing to cross their lands or recover wounded game.

As mentioned, these tribes have an intelligence and a language. Early Native Americans learned how to communicate with these tribes through rudimentary sign language, which enabled a delicate peace. Although rare, some of these encounters are documented within various tribal archives and passed along through storytelling.

As time passed, the younger members of most Native American tribes lost interest in tribal ways and lore. This was of no concern to the lost tribes, as it only furthered their ability to stay hidden. When the fur traders, gold prospectors, and settlers started to cross the tribes' lands, the tribes faced new challenges, as these humans had no understanding of the balance of nature, and they decimated vast swaths of land. Although the tribes were not originally prone to aggression, these new trespassers would have to be watched and, if necessary, dealt with. The swift retaliation delivered onto those who disrespected the lands became the way of the lost tribes, and the Native Americans who lived around these tribes started to give them a wide berth. Those who did not heed the warnings of the tribal elders would often disappear, and it was assumed the lost tribe was to blame.

Jimmy Two Horns and the rest of the tribal elders kept vigil at the base of the Hoodoo range. They could see the fire spreading as the winds swirled erratically across the ridges. The smoke moved with the winds and gave the unseen force a shape and a body of its own. The contingent of elders knew the fire crews were in trouble, not just from the fire that threatened to devour them, but also from the guardians of the forest. The elders formed a circle and began their chant. They lit more sage and herb bundles and prayed in their native tongue. They prayed for the safety of the fire crews. They prayed the fire would be contained and snuffed out. And they prayed that the guardians, the lost tribe, the Hoodoo, would see the truth in the fire crews' efforts.

They knew of the threat, as they had foreseen the possible events in a dream quest, a deep trance in which members of the council of elders could communicate with the spirits of their ancestors. This was a time-honored method for tribes to understand events to come and aid in making decisions that would best benefit the tribe. Those who were not of the tribe thought this was nonsense — superstitious hocus-pocus. Whatever one thought of this tradition, one thing was certain: Jimmy Two Horns had seen this in his dream quest, and the council respected his vision. How accurate his vision was would be proven as events unfolded. For now, prayer was all they could offer, and sometimes prayer is all that's needed.

Captain Robertson was trying to get his crews reorganized on the fire line. He could see the flames racing all along his team's firebreaks. The fire had crossed the breaks and was moving sideways along the base of the mountain as well as moving uphill.

"We gotta get an edge established on this damn fire before it burns across the entire base and surrounds us. We ain't gonna get any water drops as long as this wind is blowing like this."

Everyone knew they were on their own. The fire had jumped the access road they came in on, and a rockslide caused by spring snow melt had erased almost a mile of the only other road into the area. Construction crews repairing the damaged road had estimated it might be repaired by November. It was July, and they weren't anywhere near able to create a stop-gap solution to help the fire crews. It didn't matter anyway. The county had ordered all construction personnel and gear off of the Hoodoo range until the fire was under control. Robertson and his fire crew were effectively cut off, at least for the time being.

"Stumpy, get your crew to the north end of the fire and try to stop it from flanking us. If we can keep that corridor open, we might have an alternate way out of here down that drainage on the far side of Hoodoo."

"I'm a man down, Cap, with Slim being hurt and all. Can I grab someone from one of the other teams?"

He was hoping for Dave Wilson or Brian Frye (Spud). Both were in excellent condition and part mountain goat — valuable in this steep, rocky terrain. Having someone who could scramble quickly over steep, rocky sections could be the difference between survival and a nasty death by fire.

"You got it. Take your pick and get your ass down there."

"Thanks, Cap. Wilson, you're with me. Grab your gear, and let's roll."

Stumpy and his crew piled into the truck and headed back down the spur road. They would have to stop short and forge their own trail before they reached the main access road, as fire had control of that. That's where Wilson's ability and his saw would come into play.

Robertson ordered Ben Proctor and his team to handle the southern edge of the ever-expanding fire line and tasked Nancy Mills' team to cut an escape route over the back side of the mountain, in case it was needed.

"Nancy, I can't tell you how important it is we have a viable escape plan if this thing goes south on us." Robertson was talking in low tones close to Nancy so as not to be heard by the others. "I think we may get burned on this damn mountain. Between the fire and whatever else is up here, I got a bad feeling."

Nancy felt a chill run through her veins. She had never heard the captain sound this worried before. *Cut an escape route over the top of Hoodoo Mountain*, she repeated to herself. All she could think about was that whoever or whatever was stalking them was probably up there. After all, it was where Moore had been taken and apparently killed. At least they would be away from the fire line. It would be smokey, but at least they would be away from the heat of the flames for a while.

"You got it, John. We'll get it done."

Captain Robertson just nodded and turned to join Ben Proctor's team. Nancy turned to look over at Ben, wanting to send him a nonverbal "see you later," but Ben was already moving her way. As Ben came closer, she felt her heart racing. She wasn't sure if it was from fear of what lay ahead or nerves, because Ben seemed so intense in his gaze and stride. She was paralyzed with uncertainty of what to do or say.

"Listen, Nancy, you be careful up there. I don't want nothing happening to you. Keep your eyes peeled for anything out of the ordinary." He put his hand on her shoulder and gave her a gentle squeeze. Nancy felt the ice in her veins change to a warmth that engulfed her entire body, and, for an instant, she forgot about all that had happened that night and what was ahead of her. For an instant, she wanted to surrender to his gaze and let him swallow her up in his arms and let him hold her. For a moment.

"C'mon, Proctor, we gotta move." Captain Robertson was anxious to get to work on the problem at hand.

Reality. She snapped out of her daydream and turned to her crew.

"All right, boys, we got a road to cut."

Ben didn't want to leave so fast, but this wasn't the time. He felt the chemistry between him and Nancy too. The seriousness of the situation seemed to wake both of them up to the truth that tomorrow was promised to no one.

Nancy turned back to watch as the two trucks carrying Ben's team faded into the dust and smoke. They would be able to get to the southern end of the fire relatively quickly, as there was another spur road that broke off the one they were on and turned south. It wasn't a very good or wide road. It had been cut by the logging team for personal vehicles to access the staging areas without having to contend with larger logging trucks. Most of these roads the loggers used were barely wide enough for one truck let alone two. Many a private vehicle had been damaged or even totaled while using the roads when they would meet an oncoming logging truck with nowhere to go. The logging trucks didn't back up and rarely slowed down. Most logging operations cut the occasional passing turnout at strategic locations, but that wasn't always where vehicle meetings occurred. So, sometimes loggers would cut thin, rugged roads to their work sites to prevent precarious meetings with logging trucks. These also gave additional ways for hunters to access areas of the mountain not normally available for vehicular traffic. They were mostly utilized by hunters on four wheelers as the roads would become overgrown over time, and driving a truck on them would result in damaged paint and the occasional dent. For now, this road, freshly built this spring, was still wide enough for the fire crews to use.

Game animals also used these roads. Not only did the roads provide easier travel around the mountain, as vegetation retook the roads, they provided much needed browse for deer and other animals to feed on. With game animals using the roads, predators soon followed, and the cycle of life continued. It wasn't unusual to come around a turn on one of these improvised roads and come upon bears or other predators dining on deer or small critter right there in the middle of the road. After a couple of years, these became more like wide paths than roads, and animals felt more at ease than on the wider main roads and spurs.

As with the other animals, the tribe utilized these for easy travel through the forest while also having enough cover. And if game animals were going to use them, so would they. After all, everything has to eat.

7

THE NIGHT OF THE HOWLER

Nancy was standing watch as her crew cut their way up the mountain. She had her crew split into two teams, working a left side and a right side of what would be a rudimentary road. Cutting the trees and shrubs was relatively easy compared to moving boulders that would eat transmissions and shocks for snacks. Night was falling, and it would be darker up here away from the flames. There was an eerie, faint, red-orange glow from the fire below that punctuated the ever-growing blue-black shadows of the forest. All the crew had headlamps, and the beams of light pierced the smoke like sun rays through broken clouds. The crew was steadily moving up the mountain. They hoped to intersect the main road somewhere near the top. Even though they couldn't get out to the north, they should be able to weave their way around and down the east slope using spur roads. According to the maps, there were numerous roads winding down the east side. The only problem was, were they still viable? Most of the roads on the forestry maps had been cut years ago. They could very well be overgrown or even non-existent now.

"Hey, Spud, can you stand watch a minute? I gotta pee so bad my eyes are turning yellow." The one disadvantage of being a woman on the fire crew — can't just turn around and pee.

"Sure, boss. No problem."

Mills had spotted a good place a few yards back. She just needed to wait until the crew got a little farther up the mountain so she could have a bit more privacy. There was a large depression behind a large boulder. It was the perfect place to be out of sight. She got to the spot and was enjoying that wonderful all-familiar feeling of relief when she suddenly felt like she was being watched. She wasn't sure if it was just from being alone in the dark, or if she truly was being watched. The eerie shadows created by the red-orange glow of the fires below didn't help much. Either way, she hurried to finish and rejoin her crew. It felt like an eternity, and the short distance back to the crew seemed like a mile.

"You okay, Nancy? You look a little wide-eyed."

"I'm fine, I'm fine. Just got a lot a little spooked being so close to where Moore disappeared."

"No shit. I've had the heebie-jeebies ever since we got to that helipad. Something's out here, Nancy. And it ain't happy." Spud was another one of grounded guys not prone to superstitions or conjecture. But it was hard not to face the facts about Moore's disappearance. There wasn't anything in these woods that could snatch a man off the face of the earth. At least, not that anyone knew of. All the "accidents" with the trucks and Slim's injury added up to something far beyond their skillsets. Everyone was on edge.

"Mills! I got something up here you should see."

It was Steve Parsons. He was heading the crew working the eastern edge, the right side of the escape route.

"What ya' got, SP?"

When Nancy got to Parsons, she saw a tree that didn't look quite right. That's when it hit her. It was upside down and buried pretty deep, because it didn't wiggle at all when she pushed on it.

"What the hell? Who would go to all the trouble to do this kind of shit up here? I mean, nobody's ever gonna see that."

"That ain't all, Nance. Look at the top just below where the roots branch out." SP shone his headlamp up to where the trunk met the roots. It was an area almost hidden unless you looked for it. There it was, plain as day — a design scratched deep into the trunk. It was done a while back, too, because the patina of the wood looked old, even in the fading light. It was simple, but everyone could tell what it was. It was a face — not a complete face, just the right half. Three simple lines. One line came downward at an angle from left to right. It was about six inches long and curved back in a half oval at the bottom, forming what appeared to be an eye. The second line slightly angled from right to left and formed what could be the side of a nose. The third and last line started just to the left and below the second line and curved slightly from top to bottom. It could have been the crease that normally forms in a human face from the edge of the nose and goes outside the mouth. It was not a happy face. It looked menacing.

"What the hell—" Before Nancy could finish her thought, a deep, loud, guttural howl emanated from the shadows just below the team, not far from Nancy's potty pit. It seemed to shake the very ground they stood on and lasted almost fifteen seconds.

"Holy shit!" The whole crew froze in place, froze in fear. That howl hit their bodies like a shockwave. Whatever made that noise was close. Too close for comfort.

"All right, guys, pull in tight! Focus your headlamps in the direction of that howl."

Nancy formed her team into a defensive line with her to the side with the shotgun. Whatever was in these woods was stalking them, and she was determined not to let any of her crew get hurt.

"See anything? Anybody hear anything?"

The woods were strangely quiet, but there was something. That *smell*. It seemed to be everywhere. It was like putrid skunk mixed with that sulfurous mud smell one finds in swampy areas.

"Holy shit, Nancy! What the fuck is this thing?"

The fear in Parson's voice was echoed by the body language of the rest of the crew. Everyone was scared right down to their very cores.

Nancy just stood still, eyes fixed on the dancing shadows that permeated the dimming twilight. Time seemed to stand still. Nancy and her crew braced for whatever may come, but nothing came. It was quiet. Too quiet. The crackling from Nancy's radio made her just about jump out of her skin, and it snapped everyone back from their trances.

"Mills! Robertson here. Mills, you good up there? We heard that howling up close to your position. Over."

Nancy deftly reached for her radio, never taking her eyes off the forest around her.

"We're good, Cap. But whatever that thing is, it's close. We've stopped clearing and are in defensive positions in case it shows. Gotta tell you, Cap... we're all a little freaked out up here."

"Copy, Mills. Hang in there. How far has your team gotten, Nance?"

"We're about a quarter mile up, Cap. The road ain't very wide, and it sure ain't gonna be a smooth ride, but it's usable. Assuming we don't have any more surprises up here, we should reach the first spur road on our map shortly before sunrise. Over."

"Good work, Nance. Looks like the fire's moving faster along the southwestern edge. If Stumpy can't make good progress, I will send him and his team up your way. I don't think Mother Nature's gonna help us on this one. Wind's getting worse, and I'm not sure we'll be able to hold our line either. You may be our only lifeline, so keep plugging, but watch your back. Can't afford to lose anyone else. Out."

"Roger that, Cap. We'll keep pushing."

As if she didn't have enough problems. Cutting an escape route up steep, rugged terrain. In the dark upwind from the fire with some kind of creature or crazy person stalking her team. She would have to rally her team. The lives of every firefighter on this mountain might rely on what her and her team got done in the next several hours.

"Okay, boys, let's get back to work. We've gotta get this done. I've got your backs, but keep a eye on the forest. Shout out if you see anything out of the norm."

Her crew nervously turned back uphill and went back to work.

Everyone except Jackson Matoskah. He had to get a look at that symbol scratched into that tree.

"Jack! Where're you goin'? I need you up front."

Nancy was not happy about Matoskah deviating from the plan. Time was not a luxury they had.

"I'll be quick, boss. I need to see that tree. Something in the back of my mind. Can't quite recall it, but I think that symbol may mean something."

"Make it quick! I'll watch you, but don't dilly-dally."

"You got it, boss. I'm not thrilled about being too far from the gang with everything that's going on."

Matoskah moved quickly back to the tree. He only paused for a few seconds at the tree. When he saw the face scratched into the wood of that tree, he felt an icy chill shoot through his body. He had seen that face before. As a child, his father and grandfather would take him and his brother on camping trips into the tribal forests throughout northern Idaho. They taught the young boys woodsman skills and retold tribal stories of heroic deeds of the leaders in their tribe, and, when night had fallen and the glow of the campfire waned, they would tell of legendary creatures that inhabited the great northern forests. The Seatco, the lost tribe. Jackson and his brother, Micah, would listen to the tales of tall, hairy creatures that protected the forests from those who disrespected them — tales of inhuman strength, unnatural sounds and smells, and the territorial markings made by some of the lost tribes known to the Kalispel and other tribes.

They were told of many different types of markings — trees broken over in natural-looking but impossible configurations, boulders stacked in ways not able to be accomplished in nature, and trees planted upside down. Some of the Seatco would also carve or scratch designs into tree trunks and rocks to further identify their unique tribal territory. Cross into these areas unaware, and one could be punished. One of the designs Jackson's grandfather drew was what his grandfather called the watcher. It was three simple lines scratched into the bark of a marker tree with the sharp fingernails — or, more accurately, claws — of the Seatco. It was the same design Jackson was looking at scratched into the trunk of the upside-down tree Parsons found. He couldn't believe what he was seeing. He had always thought those stories were just that, stories — stories told to keep the young boys in line. It was easy to scare young children into obedience. There was something else in those stories, something important, but Jackson couldn't quite pull it out of his memory.

"Jack! C'mon, Jack. We gotta move it."

Nancy's bark brought Matoskah back to reality. There was work to be done, a fire to fight, and maybe, just maybe, a Seatco to face. For now, Jack would keep quiet about this. No need to stir up any more fear without a way to address it.

"Roger, boss. I'm on it."

Even as the crew made slow, steady progress up the mountain, the stench of their tormentor permeated the forest around them. It seemed to be everywhere. In front of them, behind them, flanking them. One good thing about fear — it makes one work faster. Mills' team was making good progress again. That would soon end with yet another howl piercing the darkness. This one was ahead and to the right of the crew.

"Fuck! What the hell is this thing doing? It ain't no animal. Haven't seen a critter up here. All the animals are getting the hell offa' this damn mountain 'cause of the damn fire."

SP was saying what everyone was thinking. What the hell was this thing doing? Not only that, but what the hell *was* this thing?

"Everybody, come to me! Focus your lights in the direction of that howl."

Nancy was starting to feel as though her and her team were in a battle. Not a battle with a known enemy. She was used to fighting the enemy they knew as fire, fatigue, filth, thirst, and heat. This enemy was primal, and its weapons were stealth, fear, and violence. She and her crew were unaccustomed to battling those weapons. They were ill-equipped to succeed. They had one shotgun among them and no other real weapons to defend themselves with except their youth and mental fortitude. The one thing they were totally wrong in assuming was that they were facing a single foe. In reality, they were up against several members of an ancient and hidden tribe known as Seatco to Native Americans in this area. This assumption would soon be proven wrong.

"Holy shit! There goes *another* one off to the left, ahead of us. What the fuck is going on here, Nance?"

Brian Frye (Spud), was not one to get jumpy, but his and everyone one the team's nerves were getting edgy. Even Paul Moyer, one of the few veterans on Nancy's team and normally stoic, had fear in his eyes and on his face.

All the while, Jackson Matoskah was desperately trying to recall the stories of his grandfather and father; stories, told over and over at campfires in his youth, long forgotten after years of living outside the Kalispel Tribe and its influence. He thought the old ways too mundane, filled with too much superstition and mumbo-jumbo. As he racked his brain for answers, he couldn't help but feel he'd made a terrible mistake. Maybe he should've respected his elders and stayed grounded in the old ways while spreading his wings in the white man's world — a world filled with distractions and many people without honor.

Without a sounding board of truth and knowledge, one can easily be lured onto the path blazed and bloodied by those who seek the easy ways, by those who think happiness and discovery of one's true way comes by cutting corners, using others to get to the top, cheating, lying, stealing — and, yes, sometimes killing to achieve this so-called success. As Jackson stood there in the dark surrounded by his only true friends, he realized there were no short cuts. There was only hard work, sweat, tears, and *tons* of failure. He thought that if he got out of this alive, he would re-ground his soul.

This has always been the true way of things. Tragedies and death often re-focus one's priorities. Many, however, revert back to their normal selves soon after their brush with these tests. If only he could recall the tales. There was something in there. Something about the elders and the lost tribe, the Seatco. Something about the scratching in the boundary tree. What was it? He wouldn't be able to let his mind wander for long.

Just as Nancy was going to respond to Spud, another howl split the smoke-filled shadows. This one came from below them. These howls or screams were too close together to be one creature. There was no way any one animal could move through the thick brush, and steep, rocky terrain *in the dark* without some type of giveaway — snapping a branch, kicking a rock, even a stumble. But this was not the case. Whatever it was seemed to be all around them. Surrounding them. Nancy could only think of one thing to do.

"Everybody form a circle around me! Make sure we have all headlamps and flashlights on and covering every possible angle. If anyone sees *anything* unusual, sound out!"

Nancy was about fifteen yards below the tree line in the semi-cleared escape route. She thought she had a reasonable kill zone, if needed. She grabbed her radio to call Captain Robertson for help. Maybe having more people coming up the escape route would scare away whatever was stalking them.

"Cap, come in. Cap, this is Mills. We have a situation up here. Over."

"Hey, Nance. We heard those noises down here. I've got Stevenson, Jeffries, and Davidson coming your way with the extra shotgun. Hang in there, they should be there in an hour. Can you do that, Nance? I need your team to stay focused. Looks like we're going to need that escape route... Damn fire's got us damn near flanked. Out."

"Ten-four, Cap. Out."

Only three more bodies, but at least they were bringing another shotgun. That gave her some peace of mind. But they wouldn't get there for another hour, maybe more. This was an unmapped road they were cutting, and it was rough. There would be no racing up the road. The only way to keep from bouncing into the forest or, worse, sliding sideways back down the mountain, was to move slowly but surely up the loosely packed dirt and rock-filled road.

No sooner than Nancy had signed off her radio call to Captain Robertson, it started. First, one wood knock from the forest to their left, then another from above them. Another from below, then another from the left. They came in a slow, almost rhythmic cadence at first. Then the knocks increased in number and speed, never in the same sequence. There was no left to right, right to left, or top to bottom. It was completely random. Or so it seemed to the crew. It lasted about ten or fifteen minutes, then nothing. No howls, screams, knocking — nothing. Nothing but eerie silence. Not even bug sounds. Just the wind, ever blowing thick, gray, acrid smoke up to their position. Visibility was slowly being decreased as the smoke from the fires below became even thicker. Nancy and her crew had enjoyed some "clear-air breaks," gaps in the smoke where they could get a somewhat clean breath. But now the smoke was consistent. There would be no more clean air. That was not foremost in her and her crew's minds at this moment. What was the reason for the sudden cessation of activity from their tormentors? And by now, they knew with certainty there were many. Nancy couldn't help but wonder, if one of these things could wreak so much havoc and death, what could several do? It was not a pleasant thought. After all, they didn't really know what they were up against.

Jackson Matoskah knew. He had not said anything for fear of ridicule. The others always treated him with respect. He never gave them cause to do otherwise. Oh, there was the obligatory ribbing every member of the crew got. It was part of the bonding process. It has always been the way with those who live on the edge, those who face death and injury in their duties. It was the way their mettle was tested. After all, if someone couldn't handle a little teasing, how would they handle real pressure? Jackson's Native roots did not make him immune to this ritualistic tradition. In fact, his ancestry seemed to dictate the ribbing. Terms like, redskin, Indian, and chief, among others, were sprinkled throughout conversations with Matoskah. It was part of the culture, and Jackson always took it as a sign of acceptance. He was right, but he didn't want to give his crew members any reason to doubt their trust. He didn't want the normal friendly teasing to become actual ridicule. After all, how many of them would actually take him seriously if he were to offer the explanation that they were being harassed by the Seatco, the lost tribe — large, muscular, hairy beasts of the forest. Basically, Bigfoot. And not only one, but several bigfoots. How ridiculous would that have sounded just two days earlier? How could Jackson have expected anything but to be mocked or looked at with disdain if he suggested that was behind the "accidents" and attacks. At the onset, they'd thought it might be a madman, a psycho, or something. Not Bigfoot! But things had changed, and his crewmates, his friends, were in mortal danger. He would have to tell Nancy what he knew, but he would wait just a bit longer. He didn't want to distract her from the current focus. They all needed to stay on alert at least until they knew the harassment was over and that no imminent attack was coming. He would wait.

"Anybody see anything? And I mean *anything*."

There was a quiver in her voice; everyone noticed it, but no one questioned it. No one. They all had that feeling in the pits of their stomachs. That tingling, sickly, knot-in-the-gut sensation one gets when adrenaline courses through the body, readying the body for fight or flight. *Fear*. Raw, basic, primal fear. The current situation did not allow for flight. They were surrounded. Everyone was painfully aware of the lack of options.

Nancy stood there, fixated on the direction of the loudest knock. It coincided with the loudest howl. It was the deepest howl, and the knock sounded as if it was resounding off a huge object. In her mind, this was the biggest of the things surrounding them. Maybe this was a leader or alpha. Maybe if she could get a shot at it, wound or kill it, the others would retreat. At least for a while.

This was not the way of the Seatco. There was nothing in their rudimentary language for retreat or fear. There was nothing in their culture that allowed them to pause and grieve. Theirs was a natural order: alpha male, beta male, and so on. If the alpha were killed, injured, or should die of natural causes, the beta immediately took over. Only the death of the alpha male would allow for the beta male to take the alpha female as his. This protocol had been in place for eons and served the tribe well. It ensured the survival of the tribe and rarely, if ever, varied.

Nothing moved. No noise, no sound whatsoever from the forest around them — only the smoke rushing in and the shadows flickering in the fire light from below. It went on this way for almost half an hour. No one spoke. No one moved. It was a surreal scene with the entire crew standing statue-like in a circle with Nancy in the middle, obscured by the smoke. Then, off in the distance, they heard it. A low, rumbling, mechanical sound. It was the three men Captain Robertson had sent coming up to their position.

Nancy strained her eyes downhill, looking for the headlight beams giving away the position of her re-enforcements in the smoke. The thick smoke and forest between them kept her from seeing exactly where they were. Even though she couldn't see them yet, just knowing they were close gave her and the rest of the crew some comfort. Two shotguns were better than one, and three more hands meant faster progress on the road out.

"Good God, Jeffries! You think you could *try* to miss a rock now and then. My fuckin' kidneys are gonna rupture."

Lloyd Davidson was sitting in the middle of the extended cab's back seat by himself. He jostled side to side with every bump and shift in the terrain. Arnold Stevens was riding shotgun, literally. He kept a death grip on the shotgun and had the window open to see better. Soot in the smoke coated all the windows and made visibility nearly impossible in the smokey conditions. Their headlights could only penetrate about three feet into the ever-thickening smoke. That made it difficult to see any potential obstructions, holes, or other "kidney busters." They had been driving at fair speed but now had to slow down to try and find where Mills and her crew had started cutting the escape route. Even though fresh cuts in trees and a clearer route through the timber would normally be easy to spot, the poor visibility made it easy to miss. They would have to be right on it to see it.

"Geez, Davidson, you sound like a whiney little girl. Don't wet your pants, and hang on. Gonna get rougher before it gets better."

Boyd Jeffries was one of the best off-road drivers from any of the teams. That's why Robertson sent him. He knew it would be a rough and treacherous drive and wanted an experienced driver.

"Think we missed it, Boyd? I could've sworn the road wasn't this far down this spur road."

Stevens was getting nervous. This was unlike any forest fire he'd ever been in, even without all the incidents.

Normally, they form a fire line and dig, cut, back-burn, and clean up. That's it. No driving in near zero visibility in the dark, let alone with something trying to kill them. He kept his stare out the window, never taking his eyes off the search for the escape road.

"Naw. It wasn't too far from where the road to the helipad goes up from the spur. Haven't gotten to the heliport road yet. Keep your eyes peeled."

"Whoa, whoa… I think I got it."

Jeffries hit the brakes so hard the shotgun flew out of Stevens' grip and out the window.

"Jesus, Boyd! Ya' didn't have to stomp on the brakes like that. Good thing I had my seatbelt on. I would've gone through the damn windshield. Don't move. I gotta get out and find my shotgun."

Arnold Stevens got out of the truck and stepped into a surreal world of darkness, smoke, and unknown danger. He thought the shotgun would be just out the window and by the truck, but it wasn't. It had hit the window frame on the way out, spun like a propeller, and been flung twenty feet into the shrubs ahead and to the right, just outside of the truck's headlights.

"Damn, it's hard to see out here. You guys see anything?"

Jeffries flicked the brights on, but that just created a blinding reflection that temporarily obliterated Stevens from view. When Jeffries returned his lights to normal, Stevens was nowhere to be seen.

"Where the hell are you, Arn? Arnold!"

Jeffries was getting irritated, thinking Stevens was playing games. He was known as a bit of a practical joker, after all. But this would not be funny. Too much was riding on their mission.

"You see him out there, Lloyd?"

Lloyd Davidson was leaning hard forward on the back of the front bench seat, peering through the smoke searching for Stevens.

"Man, I do t see a thing, Boyd. Let me get out and check."

"All right, but be careful. Keep your hand on the truck and stay in my headlights so I can see you."

"Roger, roger, Mom."

"I'll show you Mom, if you keep that Mom shit up. Just find Stevens, will ya'? No damn way he could've disappeared that fast. Has me kinda freaked."

Davidson made his way out of the cab and into the smoke-filled darkness engulfing Hoodoo Mountain. He gingerly stepped out towards the front of the truck, keeping himself washed in the headlights so Jeffries could see him. He shined his flashlight up the slope and into the low shrubs close to the truck, but the smoke kept him from seeing more than just a few feet ahead. Every passing second weighed heavily on both Jeffries and Davidson. They couldn't help but think about the previous night's happenings and the loss of Jesse Moore. Now, it seemed Arnold Stevens may have met the same fate.

"Got it!"

"Jesus, Arn! You scared the shit outta me. What the hell? Where've you been hiding?"

Stevens seemed to show up out of nowhere, as if beamed in. He had found the shotgun buried in the shrubbery just out of reach of the headlights. He didn't see it until Davidson's flashlight happened to shine upon it.

"Well, Mr. Worrywart, I didn't want to give my position away. There's someone or something out there, and I ain't lettin' it know where their hell I am, thank you very much."

"Okay, okay. Just get your ass back in the truck."

"Oh, by the way, the escape road *is* just a few feet back. Have Boyd back this rig on up, and I'll signal you when to stop."

"Good deal."

As Jeffries backed the truck towards the newly created escape route, Stevens waved his flashlight back and forth to guide Jeffries into position for the ascent to Mills' team.

Jeffries was watching the beam of light from Stevens' flashlight when it suddenly seemed to fly up onto the smoke-covered escape route.

Blam!

One blast from Stevens' shotgun — then silence. Jeffries floored the gas pedal and got to the last spot he had seen Arn standing. Stevens' flashlight shone across the escape route about fifty feet up the road. But there was no sign of Arnold Stevens.

"What the fuck? What the fuck?"

Davidson hung out the passenger door looking for Arn.

"Watch yourself, Lloyd! Whatever did that is still out there. You're too far out the truck. Get your ass in here!"

"In a sec, Boyd. I see the shotgun, and I'm grabbin' it."

"Be careful, buddy. Don't want to lose you too."

"Hold up right here! Got it. I don't see any sign of Arn, but there's a bunch of broken branches headin' uphill. Must've dragged him right through the bushes. Damn! There's some blood on those branches there. Son of a bitch! Son of a bitch!"

"Get your ass in here, and let's get the hell up to Mills."

Davidson jumped back in and slammed the door shut while Jeffries turned the truck onto the escape route. It was not a smooth transition. The slope was steep, and there hadn't been time for Mills and her crew to create a ramp effect for an easier transition from the spur road to the escape route. It was an abrupt change. The truck briefly lost bite on the loose dirt and rock, and started to slide into the brush where Stevens had been. Just as the truck was about to ram the shrub line, the tires grabbed hold of solid ground and the truck lurched forward uphill. Right at that moment, they felt something large land in the back of the truck.

"What the...?"

Davidson turned to shoot whatever had landed in the back.

"Go, go, go! Get this damn thing outta' here!"

It was Stevens. Somehow, he had escaped the grip of the Seatco and reached the truck before it got uphill, lunging into the bed just as the truck lurched forward. He hung on for dear life as Jeffries coaxed the truck ever farther up the mountain. When he thought they could spare some time for Stevens to get in, Jeffries stopped. Stevens deftly rolled out of the truck bed and into the open door while Davidson pulled him in and shut the door behind him, a seamless action-movie move. Jeffries jammed the truck back in gear and continued uphill.

Davidson hugged Arn with the kind of excitement only those who have cheated death would understand.

"What the hell happened, Arn? What grabbed you? You okay? You hurt?"

"I'm good. I'm good. Pretty scratched up, but I don't think anything's broken. I'm not sure exactly what grabbed me. What I know is it was *huge*, very strong, and it *stinks*. I was able to get a shot off right before the fuckin' shrubs ripped it outta' my hands. I aimed it at the arm that had me. Must've let me go 'cause of that. I do know this — that arm was huge. Bigger than any man I know. And it was hairy. Very hairy. And the hair was white."

"Wait a minute, Arn. You tellin' us there's some kinda' *monster* out there?"

"That's just what I'm sayin'. I'm startin' to think all those damn Bigfoot stories are true. It ain't no man. That's for sure."

Nancy Mills was straining to see anything of the truck carrying the three men coming to help her and her crew. She had heard the shotgun blast and, based on everything that had happened over the past couple of days, knew they were in serious trouble. The thick smoke billowing up the mountain burned her eyes and flooded her lungs. It was hard to breathe deeply, and any light coming from the incoming truck was obscured.

"Jeffries! Stevens! Come in! Over. What's your status?"

Only static came across the radio. No response from the three men in the truck.

"I repeat, status update! Are you guys all right?"

Nancy was desperate for any sign that they were okay. The whole crew surrounding her was on edge. They knew all too well that truck was probably coming up to where at least two of the wood knocks and howls had come from. They knew whatever was in these woods was nothing any of them had ever encountered, and they knew it did not want them there. To say tensions were high would be an understatement. They were all scared shitless.

"Well, guys. I'm not sure if we're getting any hel—"

"Nance, look!"

SP glimpsed a thin ray of light cut through the smoke before being choked out again. Mills strained to see what SP was seeing. Praying for the truck below to suddenly appear out of the smoke, she and her crew looked on for several seconds before another short flash of light cracked through the smoke. Then they heard it. The unmistakable sound of a Cummings NHC-250 engine heading up the road. Their reinforcements were getting close. Everyone breathed a collective relieving sigh. Not only would they have more hands on the task; they would have another vehicle available in case whatever had them on defense decided to attack. And they knew an attack was sure to come.

"Davidson to Mills. You read me? Come in, Nance! We're about a quarter mile up your way. Can you see our lights yet? Over."

"We get short flashes of light from your headlights every few seconds. You're about halfway. You guys okay? We heard a shot. Over."

"We're good, Nance. Stevens is a little beat up, but he's good. Something grabbed him and tried to take him, but he managed to get a shot off at it, and it let him go. Bruised and scratched up pretty good, but all in all, he's good. See you in a few."

Nancy and her crew exploded into cheers. They were happy for the increase in numbers, but, as those who face life and death as part of their occupation know, they were happier that the three men coming up were okay.

The radios of every crew member were set on the same frequency so everyone could hear everything coming across those radios. It kept the teams connected even when separated by great distances. This made it easier to coordinate with each other, even if the chain of command broke down. That was a good thing. But, as with all things good, there had to be a bad side — the balance of life, yin-yang, good and evil. That sort of thing. In this situation, the bad side of this instant feedback was simple. Fear. These crew members were fighting a fire, yes. But they were up against something else too. Something that had a distinct advantage over them. They heard the shotgun blast. It wasn't very close, but there was no mistaking the sound of a Remington 870 12-gauge shotgun being discharged. So everyone knew that part of their team was under attack. Until they heard the transmission between Mills and Davidson, they didn't know if those crew members were okay. This distracted the crew from their tasks at hand. Losing focus while fighting a raging forest fire could be deadly. One misstep, one slip while using an axe or a chainsaw, could result in severe injury or death. They didn't need to aide in their own demise. There would be enough of a threat from their attacker to go around.

"Focus, men! Keep your mind on your jobs. We've got a fire to fight, no matter what else is going on."

Easy to say, but Captain Robertson was having trouble keeping his mind fully on the immediate duties in front of him and his crews. He worried about everyone. They were like family to him. But he would never let them know that. His mind was on Nancy and her crew. They were in the thick of it. He heard the howls, and now he too knew there was more than one. More than one. More than one *what*? It was obvious that they were not human. He couldn't help but think about Jimmy Two Horn's words before they headed up Hoodoo Mountain.

"You will be tested. You will need to be pure of purpose. There will be death on the mountain."

Tested, Robertson understood. Pure of purpose? What the hell did that mean? And there most certainly was death on the mountain. He also recalled the words he, himself, spoke in the SITREP. *Seatco. Stick Indian. Spirit of the woods.* As he let those words drift through his mind, a chill ran down his spine, and he actually shuddered. It felt like a million degrees this close to the fire, and he got a chill. He tried to talk himself back to reality.

"Snap out of it, John! You're letting that Native American bullshit get to you."

Still, he couldn't argue with the facts of the last couple days. Injuries from unknown and unseen forces. A missing crew member and presumed death. Trucks damaged by mysterious boulders coming out of nowhere. Rocks — hell, small boulders — being thrown at his men. Something weird was on this mountain, and he needed to make sure no more of his crew fell victim. That would be a challenge, as he and his crew would find out.

Ben Proctor was having unfamiliar feelings. Feelings of dread. Not for him, but for Nancy Mills. He was worried about her. This was a strange feeling for Ben. Him and Nancy had been on many fires. They had faced deadly threats from fire, smoke, and falling debris. He had never had this feeling before. He wanted so much to radio her and tell her what he felt, to tell her he cared for her. It took all his strength to resist that urge. He could only whisper a silent prayer and hope to see her face again. Her beautiful, sparkling green eyes. Her perfect face. He wanted to hold her, to keep her safe. He wanted to kiss her. At that moment, he realized it. He was smitten. He resigned himself to tell her exactly how he felt the next time he saw her. What if he never saw her, again? What if she fell victim to another attack from... from *what*? He got that sick feeling in the pit of his stomach. He may never see her alive again. If he did, he would *not* waste the opportunity.

Carter (Stumpy) was thinking about everything that was happening too. He and his crew were closer to Nancy's position than the other teams, but it was just his crew. Robertson had Proctor's crew plus additional manpower from his crew and the captain. Stumpy knew he needed to keep doing his job. The fire wasn't progressing as fast at his position as it was over at Proctor's location. But that could change with the wind. They would have to hold their line so all the teams could make it to the escape route Mills was cutting. It might be their only chance at surviving.

Stumpy had heard the howls and the knocking, and he, too, was now aware that there was more than one attacker. It hit him out of the blue: *Seatco*. What the hell was a Seatco? Those words that he half-heartedly listened to during the SITREP. *Spirit of the woods.* One thing was certain — whatever was attacking the crews was no spirit. It was flesh and blood. But what kind of flesh and blood?

They would all know soon enough. There would be no doubt as to what was in these woods. And they would be tested and would need to be pure of purpose.

It had been sleeping for most of the day, resting for what would be done that night. The tribe was resting, satisfied by the meal it had provided. They only ate when they needed to. There was no such thing as three squares a day. One good meal would carry them for a day or two, even though these beings were very large. Big ones could approach ten feet tall and over 800 pounds. Their metabolism was such that any meal fed their muscles, keeping them operating like machines. There wasn't much fat in their diet, so they were not prone to disease. They rested when needed, usually during the day to keep from being seen. They hunted at night when larger prey animals typically moved. They would normally ambush their prey along proven game trails. If need be, they would operate in teams of two or three to push potential game towards an ambush location, but the alpha normally hunted alone. Their smell gave them away, so more than one could jeopardize a hunt. Prey animals are adept at avoiding predators.

While it lay there in the protected cavern system they occupied, it could smell the increasing smoke from the fires. It was not affected by that at all, as the cavern system had cross-breeze ventilation formed by natural effects from erosion coupled with dug-out egress points for stealthy exits from their lair. It knew the trespassers were not as equipped to deal with the dark as they were. It also knew they had split into three groups. They didn't have a real language, not by man's definition anyway. But they did communicate. While the alpha slept, the subservient took turns watching. They would communicate to the alpha any changes he needed to be aware of. The invaders that moved up the mountain were getting too close to finding one of their entrances. They couldn't afford to let them discover their home, so the entire tribe would be used to defend it.

They knew what to do; they had been there before. Although it was rare for all the male members of the tribe to be involved, it had happened before, and the victims were now part of the mysterious disappearances surrounding the mountain. This one would be more difficult. There were many more trespassers this time. But they knew, instinctively, what to do. Surround, harass, attack the weak points to diminish their numbers, and remove the trespassers in a way that the humans could not be found. And always operate in the dark, where they had the advantage. This was their tactic, and it had served the lost tribes of the world for eons, with rare exception.

They would start with the group closest to their home and work down to the others. The males all left the safety of the caverns and made their way to their understood positions. It was instinct; there were no orders, no oral communication. The alpha, the biggest and strongest of the males, would be at the front of the trespassers and would signal the start with a signal howl — long, loud, and resonating as deeply as he could muster. He would be fairly close to the trespassers to shock them and strike fear deep into their hearts. He would try to keep them from advancing farther up their territory. The next two strongest males would position below to try to keep the trespassers from escaping and keep other trespassers from coming up. The flanks would be handled by the youngest of the "of age" members, mainly to make noise and throw rocks.

They were not to engage the enemy, because they were not deemed worthy yet. This challenge would be part of their initiation into larger responsibilities within the tribe. But the killing would be left to the hunters of the tribe. They knew how to kill quickly and what to do with the bodies. They had the strength to accomplish their mission. The flankers, the younger males, would not be allowed to come in actual contact with the offenders. It would be too risky for the tribe. But, as with young males in human society, sometimes the young did not obey. It seemed to be a universal truth that mammals tested the limits. This is what had happened when one of the flankers had attempted to grab Stevens. The trespasser had gotten so close. It would have been easy to grab the man and take him to an elder male for punishment. As with young males of the human species, testosterone overcame wisdom, so he attacked the human. The human was so close, and he knew he was stronger based on sheer size alone. So he had attacked. He had the human by the waist and was dragging him through the thick undergrowth of shrubs and pine saplings. It was easy. The human was light compared to the boulders and trees he had handled in his short life. He barely felt it struggle. He knew he was not to engage the humans. He was there just to herd them to the elders. But, surely the elders would be happy to see him take a prize, to eliminate a threat to the tribe. He just didn't count on the weapon the human had. He had never experienced weapons other than stones or stumps. He'd thought the human just had a stick in his hand, and a puny one at that — too small to inflict harm upon his muscular frame. It had surprised him when the loud blast came from that small stick and further shocked him to see the damage such an insignificant stick had inflicted on his arm.

His arm was nearly severed just above the wrist, and the pain caused him to release his hold on the human. Not only had he violated his standing in the tribe, he was hurt and pretty badly. This would not end well for this flanker. He knew he might be banished from the tribe, and with an injury such as this, survival would be difficult. Worst of all, his flanking position had been compromised, leaving a gap in their defenses. He would fight the pain and bleeding and find a place to hide that would allow him to stay somewhat in position. It was all he could do. That, and wait for his punishment.

The alpha had heard the shotgun too and knew all too well what kind of damage it could do to flesh. It had seen deer and other large game that had been wounded by the weapons of man and survived the initial trauma only to perish of those wounds later. The meat was never wasted. The tribe would scavenge it, and the carcasses would feed the coyotes, wolves, cougars, and birds of the forest. All would be used by all. But the lack of respect — who would wound an animal and not make every effort to retrieve it? It did not go unnoticed by the tribe. They saw or heard all that happened within their territory. They rarely intervened in those encounters, for the tribe was opportunistic when it came to food. The easier to get, the better. Wounded animals were easy meals, so they would simply do what they did. Watch and wait. He had heard the blast of the shotgun and knew it was close to one of the young flankers, but there was no way for him to know if the flanker was injured or not. That would be sorted out when the group regathered in the caverns. For now, there were trespassers to deal with. Trespassers who continued to tear apart their forest with their smelly tools, laying waste to their precious trees in mere seconds, whose fumes were more noxious to them than the smoke from the fires approaching their home.

They were not worried about the fire. They had seen it before. The safety of their caverns would protect them, and the forest always rebounded quickly after fire. It was the destruction caused by these humans that left a more permanent scar upon the land. Once humans forged a path in the forest, other humans would traverse it, at least for a while. It allowed more and more humans to access their lands, hunt their food, and disrespect their ways.

Not all humans were like this. They had seen and, yes, even interacted with some in the distant past who had treated the land and the beasts within with the same respect and reverence they did. But this was getting rarer. In fact, there had been no interaction between any living members of this tribe and humans. It seemed, most humans who entered their land treated it and the animals that called it home as if they were not important. They left behind all manner of trash and left their mark on almost everything they touched. They painted rocks with strange markings, something the tribe took as marking territory, an attack of sorts on the tribe's very claim. They made small fires and would leave them smoldering when they left. Always, the tribe watched and waited. Sometimes, they tried to scare the trespassers off with howls, wood knocks, and rocks thrown close to the humans. Sometimes, they would just wait for them to leave.

Once the humans left, they would go in and roll the offending boulders over to cover the markings. They knew of fire and its characteristics from eons of experiences, so they would place large boulders on top of the smoldering pits to contain the embers. They knew nothing of glass, metal, and plastic, so cans, bottles, and other things left behind stayed where they were, creating a lasting reminder to the tribe of the unworthiness of these offenders to enter their lands peacefully. All these experiences with humans would culminate in the tribe unleashing rage upon the most egregious of those tres-passers. Tonight was one of those times.

The alpha saw the lights from the trespassers' vehicle moving ever further into their lands. It knew there should be two flankers on each side of the newly cut hole in their forest and one below. As the truck progressed, the flankers would stay parallel and move up with the truck while the rear guard kept pace. This would tighten the circle around the trespassers until all were within the kill zone. The alpha would wait for the truck.

"Robertson to Stumpy! Come in, Sam! Over."

Stumpy was wondering if Robertson had forgotten about them.

"Go for Stumpy, Cap! What ya' got?"

"Fire's closing in on us fast. Don't think we can hold this line much longer, and I don't like what I hear up towards Mills' location. I think we're gonna' trickle out of here three or four at a time. We've got the extra truck, so we'll move personnel from here to Mills' twenty. We'll gather your team up with the last load. Over."

In first responder parlance, twenty meant location. Everything had a code. It made for quicker communication, and time was always of the essence.

"Ten-four, Cap! We'll hold out as long as we can. Over."

"Ten-four, Stumpy. Out."

"Okay, Toothless, take Gordon, Hightower, and Yancey and head up to Mills. And watch your asses. I've got a bad feeling about all this bullshit."

"You got it, Cap."

Frank Welch, aka Toothless, felt the same way. He had been there when Moore disappeared and knew they were in for a rough night. Between the fire and whatever was after them, he felt they would have to keep their wits about them if they were to come out of this alive. He didn't like that the only weapons on them were axes, shovels, picks, and the small knives they all carried for menial cutting tasks. Not much good in a fight. Robertson and Proctor needed the two shotguns, because they were now reducing their ranks, which could open them to attack. He and the other guys would have to make do with what they had, if need be.

"It's gonna be tight, but everyone rides in the cab. I don't want anyone exposed in the back. Let's get in there, boys."

Toothless was right to have everyone in the cab. It would provide some cover from the type of attacks they had experienced so far. Boulders, smaller rocks, tree stumps, and logs could all damage the truck, but they would crush a man. Plus, it would be a very rough ride, and it would be difficult to fall out of the cab.

Everyone loaded into the truck, and in just a few seconds, it was on its way to Mills.

"Robertson to Mills. Come in. Over."

"Mills here. Go ahead, Cap. Over."

"I got a truck heading' your way with some more reinforcements. We're losing our battle at this twenty, so we are going to trickle retreat. Toothless is bringing Gordon, Yancey, and Hightower. They should be there within the hour. Out."

"Ten-four, Cap. I owe you one. Out."

Nancy had hoped to hear Ben Proctor's name on that list, and it gave her a sinking feeling when she didn't. At least he would be coming soon, she hoped.

Not long after talking with Robertson, the first reinforcements made it to her and her crew, and she felt a wave of relief roll over her.

Arnold Stevens rolled out of the cab first, and he looked a sight. He was scratched up pretty badly, and his clothes were torn a bit. That was what struck Nancy. Fire crew clothes were almost bulletproof. It would take quite a feat to tear them.

"You okay, Arn? You look like you've been in a battle."

Stevens had that focused, serious, stare on his face. Normally, these fire crews would laugh off near-death events and move on. Not now. Stevens was visibly shaken.

"Nance. I gotta' tell ya', I ain't never seen anything like what I saw tonight. I'm tellin' ya', it's a damn creature of some kind, and it's *huge*."

Huge. Stevens hadn't seen huge yet. What grabbed him was a mere six feet five inches or so. Maybe weighing about 250 or 300 pounds. The alpha was pushing eight feet tall and 800 pounds.

"What're you talkin' about, Arn? A monster or something? You're sounding like you're in shock."

"All I can tell ya' is what I saw. I shot the damn thing in the arm, and it was the biggest arm I've ever seen, and it was covered in whitish-gray hair. And the hands — . the hands were like claws."

Nancy didn't want to believe what she was hearing, but it was hard to argue with the facts as she knew them. Damaged trucks, injured and missing crew members, and the howls and wood knocks. She had heard the stories before. Everyone had heard the stories. Bigfoot, Sasquatch, whatever. But she always believed they were just that, stories. Fun to tell with no truth in them whatsoever. But now it was different. It was happening to her and her crew. Must have been some truth in the stories.

"What about you two? You see any monsters out there?" Mills intentionality used a slightly sarcastic tone to ease the tension. Davidson and Jeffries weren't sure exactly what they saw. It had all happened too fast, and neither was about to get labeled a kook.

"Didn't really get a good look at it, Nance. I was focused on driving. Could've been a bear." Jeffries knew it wasn't a bear but wasn't going to say different.

"A damn big bear. If it was a bear." Davidson also knew it wasn't a bear, but, for now, a bear it was.

Anderson wasn't so cautious about being labeled. He knew that whatever grabbed him was definitely not a bear.

"A bear, my ass! I'm tellin' you, it's some kinda creature."

"Okay, guys. Let's not lose our grip. We got a fire to fight. Head over and get some water, then grab your gear. We've gotta get this trail cleared best as we can. It may be our only way outta here."

Jackson Matoskah overheard Stevens' report to Mills and figured now was his chance to tell her what her knew. At least, what he thought he knew.

"Nance, can I talk to you for a sec over here? I got something to tell you."

It was rare for Matoskah to do much talking. He usually kept his thoughts to himself. So when he asked to talk, she wanted to listen.

"Sure, Jack. What you got?"

"I think I know what we are dealing with here, boss. It's the Seatco. The Kalispel have known of the Seatco for hundreds of years. Loosely translated, it means *stick Indian*, as in the Indians who live in the forest. My grandfather and my father told me and my brother stories of the Seatco when we were young. We thought it was more or less a boogie man story. But now, I think I was wrong. The Seatco is real. It is said to guard this mountain, and even the name Hoodoo means devil or beast. There are even stories about the Hoodoo Howler. Explains the howls we've been hearing, huh? I have hunted this mountain and have had some weird feelings up there at times, but I never thought it was anything but my nerves."

"Not you, too. Are you tellin' me there's some sort of a devil on this mountain, Jack? You can't be serious about that, can you?"

"Not so much devil as beast, Nance. It is said that it is the guardian of the mountain and will punish those who disrespect the natural ways. I wasn't convinced until I saw it. You know that upside-down tree with that weird scratched design on it? That is how the Seatco marks its territory. My grandfather drew that very design in the dirt to show us, so we would know if we had entered the Seatco's lands. You have to understand this, Nance. If what my people say is true, these 'guardians' are more like a tribe than a pack. They have an intelligence of sorts and are here to protect their lands from those who would destroy them. It looks like they think we are a threat to them, and that's why we've been attacked."

"Jack, we've done nothing but try to save this forest, to protect this mountain. If this, whatever, has an intelligence, don't you think it would know that or sense that?"

I don't know, Nance. But we are cutting the trees, setting fires, and changing the landscape. Could be misunderstood as destruction. It would explain the missing brothers. They set this fire with their fireworks, and now we're doing the same thing. Kinda makes sense, if you think about it."

"Holy shit, Jack. If what you're saying is true, we're in for some serious shit. Is there anything in those stories of yours that tells us how to fight or stop them? That would be a lot more helpful than, 'Hey everybody, we're fighting goddamn monsters up here.'"

"I think there's something, but I can't remember. I was pretty young when I was told those stories. But, still, I think there is something in the back of my mind, and it's driving me crazy."

"Well, keep trying, Jack. All our lives may depend on what you might know."

"Yes, ma'am. I'll keep trying."

It was about to give the signal to attack, when it heard something below off in the distance. It drew in deep breathes through his nose, trying to get the scent. It strained to hear. It didn't take long to realize there was another one of those smelly machines, likely bringing more trespassers up here. Soon, there might be too many to fight. One fire stick was bad, now there were two; that's worse, and there soon may be more. It did not want to risk the future of the tribe by risking the lives of the flankers. They were too young to fully understand the dangers of the fire sticks and were not fully trained in the ways of the fight.

As the alpha stood there, surveying the scene around him, he thought about the other trespassers on these lands. Maybe they could move the attack to the others. He would need to scout and see which group to attack first. The fire was moving, and he would have to move quickly.

He signaled for the beta with two wood knocks. The beta was second in the tribal hierarchy and would be stationed in the alpha's position while the alpha scouted out the other offenders. It was his responsibility to decide what the tribe would do, and the tribe would follow the alpha's lead. He would go to the trespassers he knew were farthest away. They would be most vulnerable to attack. The ones nearest the fire. Team A's location. There would not be another attack on these offenders until he decided which group to attack. He had to be sure the tribe would not suffer losses. These tribes were small, and any member lost would take years to replace. Once the beta was in place, he made his way to the trespassers below.

Fire is dynamic. It moves along the path of least resistance, pushed by the wind and available fuel. Little did Captain Robertson and Team A know, the fire had flanked them about a mile to their south. The spur road was impassable, and their battle to slow the fire on the south side was futile. The only way they would get off the mountain rested in the hands of Mills and her crew's ability to create a hole in the woods for the trucks to get through.

"It's gettin' pretty hot in here, Cap. With this wind, I don't think we've got much time."

Ben Proctor was right. They only had about two hours until the fire would close off their escape down the north section of the spur road. After that, the only way out would be straight up the mountain through the thick brush and rocky outcrops. Not an ideal path to take, and they would have to go on foot. There was no way to get a vehicle up that way.

"Okay, Ben, I think we better start planning our retreat. When Toothless gets back, we'll send three more guys out, and, assuming the fire cooperates, we'll continue with that until everyone's out. Shouldn't take more than a couple hours. If we can slow the progress of the fire enough, it might buy Mills time to reach the upper road or at least get close enough to make a charge for it. I got a feeling it's gonna' get rough here real soon."

"Sounds like a plan, Cap. I just hope we can hold the line long enough. That wind's really starting' to swirl."

As Robertson watched the truck's taillights disappear into the smoke, he felt a chill of dread creep up the back of his neck. He sensed something lurking just out of sight somewhere in the woodland shadows. He couldn't explain it; it was just a feeling. He stood there almost frozen, his gaze fixed on the tree line behind his crew.

He was the type of man that didn't scare easy, and he was very much aware of his vulnerability and the fragility of human life. As he stood there engulfed in smoke and the red-orange glow of the fire, everything faded from the forefront of his mind, and an eerie quiet crept into his mental wanderings. It didn't last long. This was no time for losing focus on the task at hand.

"Cap, you okay? You look like you're somewhere else."

Ben Proctor felt the same uneasiness in the air, but they had other immediate worries. The fire was moving fast, and they needed to keep their escape route clear.

Ben's voice snapped Robertson out of his funk, and he turned back to the fire.

"Let's get some space in here for us to move back up the spur road. We can't let the fire cut us off."

Proctor got his crew redeployed from suppressing the fire to maintaining their escape lane. It was a major disappointment to the crew. They weren't used to giving in to the fires they faced, but this was an extraordinary event. High winds, plenty of bone-dry tinder, and an unknown assailant stacked the odds against them. The crew would fight to survive the night and try to regroup at a higher fire line. The city of Priest River could depend on it.

Toothless could see the tire tracks where SP's truck had turned up the escape route.

"What a fuckin' mess. This ain't no road. It's a goddamn goat trail."

Toothless was on edge. He and the others had heard the shotgun blast too. Someone had shot at something right where they were, so his senses were on hyper alert.

"Keep your eyes peeled, fellas. These woods are hidin' somethin,' and I don't want to meet it. Know what I'm sayin'?"

No one said anything. They were all thinking the same thing. Time seemed to slow down. It's like that when fear grabs hold. The heart speeds up, the tingling in the pit of the stomach heightens, eyes widen, all the senses go into overdrive, and the brain seems to act like a slow-motion camera, creating a feeling of slowing time. This helps the body respond quickly to any threat. Everybody has a different response to this surge of sensory input. Some freeze, others have an overwhelming need to run, and others face the threat and fight. First responders are trained to know which of these commands to obey, and the fight response is the logical choice in most situations. So, as Toothless maneuvered the truck up the rugged escape route, everyone in the truck was poised to react, ready for an assault from an unknown attacker but hoping they would not have to fight. Every foot covered on that trail was agonizingly slow. Every slip of the tires froze their hearts as they braced for the worst.

The road was barely wide enough for the truck, and the forest seemed impossibly thick and dark. Nancy's crew had done as good a job clearing a way as they could with the tools they had and the terrain they confronted. Because of the thick smoke, the beams from the headlights only reached a few feet up the road. Large rocks in the road were almost impossible to avoid due to the lack of visibility, punishing the truck's suspension and tires with every contact.

"Holy shit, Toothless! Slow the fuck down! We want to get there in one piece."

Yancey was voicing what the others were thinking. How much of this pounding could this truck take? No one wanted to be hiking up this narrow road in the dark with a predator in the area. Not only that, the truck would need to make this trip several more times. But these trucks were built for military use and could take a lot of abuse. But being built for survivability meant these trucks sacrificed comfort. The men in it felt every bump and bang deep in their core, but the truck would be okay.

"Don't worry, guys, these trucks were made for this. Just grab something and hang on. Can't be much farther."

Hearing Toothless and the others coming up the road gave Nancy and the others even relief, and she felt she could lower her guard a little. There hadn't been any more howls or knocks for over an hour, and the awful smell had faded. But she wasn't sure if that was because of the smoke. Smoke can camouflage odor.

The alpha repositioned the tribe to the southeastern side of the trespassers and would wait there until the beta returned. This put it and the tribe between two of the groups of trespassers, and they would easily be able to move to the lower group of humans if they found it easier to attack them instead. The last member of the tribe to gather with the alpha was the wounded young male. By now, he had gnawed the nearly severed hand free and had packed the gaping would with moss, mud, and his spit. It still hurt, but the wound would not hinder its ability to perform its responsibilities to the tribe. The alpha approached the juvenile and glared long and hard into its eyes. Normally, the price of disrespect was banishment from the tribe. There was no court system, no written laws. There was only the hierarchy of the tribe. All members knew their place and understood the consequences of disobedience. The juvenile lay prostrate on the ground before the alpha and waited for the alpha's wrath. It didn't come. The alpha needed every male member to attack the trespassers, even a young, wounded juvenile. Instead, the alpha grabbed the offending male by the scruff of its neck and lifted it off the ground. The juvenile would be marked with a long gouge along its cheek. It was a warning. One more mistake would mean banishment without exception. It would serve as a reminder to the juvenile of its place for as long as it lived. In the wisdom of the tribe's ways, it would keep it from making another similar mistake later. It would also remind the rest of the tribe of the youth's warning in case the alpha were to die and another take its place. The law of the tribe and the alpha's judgement would be carried out as if the alpha was still alive if the member failed again. The tribe would remain whole, for now.

The beta watched the trespassers from the forest shadows just above them. Its keen night vision allowed it to see even the ones beyond the light. They were moving. Moving in the direction of the others. If the tribe was going to attack this group, it would need to do so before they reached the others. It watched for several minutes, making sure of the trespassers' moves before rejoining the rest of the tribe. If these offenders continued to diminish in number, they would be easier to eliminate. But that would mean the other trespassers would grow in size. Timing would be important to the tribe's success.

Mills refocused her efforts on clearing an escape route. With the added help, she hoped to make better forward progress, and with more help on the way, she felt fairly confident they could reach one of the logging service roads above. Assuming the service road wasn't too overgrown, and assuming whatever was in these woods left them alone, and assuming the fire didn't pick up too much speed, they should make the first service road by dawn. Nancy knew full well that that was a lot of assuming.

"All right, boys, let's clear the road."

Mills felt rejuvenated by the added bodies. She took up a position with the lead cutters and put Stevens at the back of the group with his shotgun. She needed to make sure nothing came up behind them, and Stevens could use the rest after his brush with the creature.

"Davidson, stay close to Stevens so he's got an extra set of eyes. Whatever is out there is *still* out there somewhere, and I don't want anybody else getting hurt."

"Ten-four, Nance. Nothin's gonna get by us."

Stumpy and his crew were working close to a major drainage on the northwestern slope of the mountain. He was lucky that the area had a large swath of boulders from an ancient avalanche, and there was very little fuel in that area. This gave his crew a safe-zone cushion if the fire picked up speed. That was the good news. The bad news was it was a very steep slope with treacherous footing. It would be easy to sprain an ankle or even break a leg. On top of that, their only truck was up Mills' escape route. Stumpy and his crew would go on foot if they had to bug out before Robertson's truck picked them up. It gave Stumpy an extreme sense of isolation. He and his crew were vulnerable to the mountain, the fire, and whatever was on this mountain with them. It gave him a heightened sense of his surroundings, almost as if he were tuning in to something primal. A sixth sense or something. He couldn't explain it, but he sensed a change in the environment. He scanned the skyline, the smoke plumes, and he strained to see if the fire lines below him were much different. Everything seemed as expected, but he couldn't help but feel something was off. He shook his head and told himself to snap out of it. It almost struck him as funny hearing those words in his head; something felt off. Holy crap! The whole damn situation was off. For the time being, he would stick to the plan and keep the northwest flank of the escape route open. But something seemed to whisper in his ear, "Keep your head on a swivel and your eyes wide open." Stumpy would need the silent warning.

The beta rejoined the tribe and gave the alpha the report on the trespassers. They had a language, but not like humans do. It was a combination of vocalizations, hand gestures, and rudimentary drawings in the dirt. It was a more visual language, using symbols and shapes to identify landmarks, locations, game, and threats. They had a working knowledge of the areas surrounding their lands, the areas occupied by the humans. Those lands were identified as a series of squares and rectangles, with food sources marked with small and large circles indicating small or large food items. They also indicated those who would be protected from attack, as shown by the symbol of the tribe — the three lines that formed the face. That marking had not been used since the time before the smelly machines. There was a time when humans only entered these tribal lands on foot or horseback. Those humans understood and respected the tribe and its ways.

It had been several lifetimes since those days, and if not for the tribe's symbolism in drawings, that would have been erased from its memory, much like how modern Native Americans seem to avoid the ancient ways and traditions. If not for the written and oral teachings handed down from elder to elder and retold at pow-wows, annual gatherings of the different Native tribes, and other Tribal meetings, the old ways would have been lost forever. As it were, they were a distant, foggy memory buried deep in the subconscious of most modern day Natives. Such was the information buried in Jackson Matoskah's memory.

The information the beta brought back proved the alpha had been correct to halt the initial attack. The alpha's role as provider, protector, and punisher was complicated. Mistakes could mean injury or the death of tribal members. After all, one in the tribe had already suffered a severe injury, and they could ill afford any losses to their numbers. This was the downside of keeping the group's numbers small. The loss of even one member would take years to replace.

The alpha looked at the group of males in front of him and indicated his decision. They would attack the lower offenders and, once they were gone, the tribe would move to attack the others. The attack would be simple. They always were. Surround, confuse, harass, isolate, and then eliminate them. It was always the same. Use the shadows to gain position, use the tools around them, and don't leave any signs behind.

They were good at this, as human history proved. The only evidence of the tribe's existence was in local legends, Native tales, and suspect evidence. Even clear evidence of their presence had always been doubted and rebuked by a skeptical human population, so sure of their precious superiority in the universe that there couldn't possibly be anything unknown in their world. They were too intelligent and too enlightened to fall for ancient knowledge, folklore, or campfire stories. If there wasn't a body, it couldn't possibly exist. That smugness is what normally got the humans into trouble. If they would know, understand, and respect the rules of nature and life, there would be no need to fear the dark. But the nature of most humans is one of superiority and dominance. Rather than find harmony in the natural ways of the world, they seek to bend the world to their own devices. This causes disharmony and unbalance in nature.

The ironic thing about trying to change nature is that nature cannot be changed. Oh, it can temporarily fall prey to the will of mankind, but nature always returns to nature. After all, how many ancient and highly developed human cultures have existed, thrived, and then faded into oblivion., leaving their cities, culture, and technology to be swallowed by the forests or even the earth itself? It has happened time and time again, and until humans learn from this, they will always suffer the same fate. Extinction of the culture and elimination of the physical evidence. Sometimes this extinction is due to poor placement of their cities, such as building too close to volcanos, earthquake zones, or coastlines that are subject to tsunamis or severe storms. Or, as with the tribe, justice is meted out for disrespecting the nature that surrounds them. This might not result in a cultural extinction, but it did result in the extinction of that life. And, as far as the tribe knew, that was all that mattered. The culture of the tribe was not one to be discovered. Theirs was a culture born in mystery and would not be subjected to the intellectually misguided humans bent on furthering their own superiority. That was not the natural order of things.

The male tribe members moved quickly and silently towards the offenders below. Each knew its role in the attack to come. The subordinate members would position on each side of the trespassers while the alpha placed himself above. Once each was in position, it would signal with a short whoop. Once all were in position, the alpha would signal the attack with a long, bellowing, howl meant to freeze the offenders with fear and confusion. This gave the tribe a moment to inflict the most damage before the humans could take cover or fight back. The tactic was a proven one. They had done this time and time again for millennia.

They hunted this way as well. Large game would first freeze in place, hoping to avoid being seen. While it stood still, a member of the tribe would either kill it with a well-placed rock throw or chase it down and break its neck. No matter the method, the result was the same. The animal was dead, and the tribe would eat. With offending humans, it was more visceral. Not only would the human be killed, it would be quickly dismembered. The tribe did not eat the kill; that was left to the coyotes, birds, and other carnivores. The tribe would not eat the offenders, for they were not deemed edible. Something to do with a poisoned soul creating poisoned meat. As mentioned, they had a language but not one humans could grasp. Theirs was a society based upon a simple purity, albeit a violent and sometimes grotesque belief; it was based on a basic understanding of the tribe's definition of which actions were right and which actions were to be punished. There was only one punishment, and that was death, and death was coming to these current offenders.

"You hear that, Cap?"

Ben Proctor heard it. Like a low roar. The sound fire makes when it's surging. That sound was like no other sound in nature, and it meant the fire was gaining ground, large chunks of ground. The worst part was it came from behind them between their position and the escape route. The wind had continued to pick up, and as it blew up the mountain, it knocked down the beetle-damaged trees in large swaths. The fire greedily fed on the new fuel and raced along the trees so fast it almost looked like they were fuses, burning towards new stands of timber well past the backfires and firebreaks. The rush Ben Proctor had heard was several large dead trees falling across the spur road and being engulfed by flames. Mills' team might not only need to cut an escape route, but also cut across the top of the mountain and create a fire break by dropping trees in the direction of the fire to keep the fire from crossing the ridge and heading down towards the town of Priest River.

Robertson heard the sound too. He turned towards it and saw the red-orange glow of the fire as it bounced off the smoke, punctuated by flames reaching skyward amid the embers blowing in the wind. It was only a quarter mile away, and he knew they were cut off from the escape route, as did every one of the crew. They knew there was only one way out now, straight up Hoodoo Mountain. It would be a desperate run. Fire burns faster uphill than down. Faster than a man can run. Their only chance was to make it to the rocky outcrop a quarter mile up in the hopes the rocks would provide enough cover from the flames for them to survive. A slim chance at best. Many a fire crew had been lost by trying to outrun a fire uphill.

"Fuck! Proctor, get the crews off the fire line and bring 'em here. I'll radio the other teams and let them know what's up."

"Ten-four, Cap. It ain't gonna be pretty."

Proctor's heart sank at the thought of their predicament. Odds were not in their favor. The only way they had a chance was to go light. No unnecessary equipment — that would only slow them down. Axes, survival tent, water. This time, they would also need the shotguns and ammunition. They weren't just trying to outrun a fire; they might have to fight their way to safety as well.

"Mills, Stumpy! Robertson here. Listen, we're bugging out up the mountain. The fire's cut off our route to the escape. We're gonna head for the rock outcrops up top. Hope to hunker down and let the fire blow over us. Stumpy, get your team to Nancy's twenty. You get your teams up to the crest and clear one of those access roads, then split into two teams. One to the north and the other to the south to try and cut off this damn fire before it heads to Priest River. After the fire burns over us, we'll try and rendezvous with whoever goes south. Good luck, people. Robertson, out."

The news hit Stumpy and Mills hard. Especially Mills. She knew the odds of outrunning an uphill fire. She couldn't help but feel she'd lost her chance to tell Ben how she felt. She felt she would never see him again. But there was no time to waste on self pity or sorrow. If Ben and the other crew members survived the fire somehow, it would be her team there to greet them when they crossed the ridge.

Captain Robertson gathered his crewmen and filled them in on their situation. Even though they all knew the odds, not a single crewman showed any sign of fear. They had a trip to make, a mountain to climb, and a fire to beat.

The crews started their ascent of Hoodoo Mountain. It was slow going in the dark, and the terrain was rugged with thick growths of scrub pines and Douglas firs. The thick smoke hindered the use of their flashlights. Even with the lights, visibility was only a few feet in front of them.

The tribe heard the sound too and saw the fire's glow moving up the mountain. The tribe knew fire. They had been through fires before. Their mountain was covered in old, charred stumps and broad clearings caused by previous fires. They also knew their cave would protect them when the time came. They would move to attack the lower offenders, and if they didn't succeed in eliminating all of them, they knew the fire would finish the task.

"Time to giddy up, boys. Focus on those boulders, and don't look back."

The urgency in Robertson's voice put everyone into automatic overdrive. They gathered their gear and started up the mountain, hoping to reach the relative safety of the boulder outcrop above them. Rocks don't burn, and it would be the best place to set up their emergency fire protection tents. Although the tents were not prone to burning and reflected a great deal of heat, the human body can only tolerate so much before cardiac arrest or severe heat stroke became a real danger to the fire fighters. The boulder outcrop would prevent the fire from burning close to the crew, keeping the intensity of the fire from cooking them. Hopefully.

The crew picked their way up the steep, boulder-strewn mountainside, moving with the almost superhuman strength and focus that adrenaline provides through the fight-or-flight reflex. This was definitely flight mode, and they were making their way up the mountain with good speed. They moved so fast and were so focused on their destination that no one noticed the boundary markers of the tribe as they climbed ever higher. Granted, it was dark, and the upside-down tree markers were placed in strategic locations so as not to be overtly seen, but if one was looking, they could be easily identified. Even if the markers had been noticed, they would not have registered with anyone as a warning. With the fire chasing them down, it wouldn't have mattered anyway.

Robertson led the crew, with Ben Proctor bringing up the rear. Robertson set the pace, and Proctor made sure no one fell behind. Injury and overexertion were real possibilities on this climb, and having a man like Ben Proctor watching everyone's back gave the crew some confidence that they would all make it to the boulders and have a fighting chance at survival. That feeling wouldn't last long. It happened at a point in the climb where the fire fighters had to turn sharply to their left to avoid a sheer drop of a hundred feet or so. Proctor could see the light from the lead crew members turn into the wood line and disappear as they snaked their way through the thick forest. They would have to make their way back to the edge of the tree line where it was more open and easier to move. He could see the man in front of him, George Ludlow.

Ludlow was only twenty or thirty feet in front of him when a basketball-size rock struck him in the chest. The blow knocked Ludlow off his feet, and he was thrown over the edge of the drop-off, and he was gone. He was hit with such force that he wasn't even able to scream. The only sound Proctor heard was what he could only think was bones breaking when the rock hit him. He knew Ludlow was gone, but he instinctively raced to the edge to try and find him. The cliff dropped off into a deep ravine that looked bottomless in the darkness. Not even the glow of the fire lit the bottom. It was as if Ludlow had just been swallowed up by the mountain.

"George! George!" Proctor's calls went unanswered, and a sick, sinking feeling overcame him.

"Where the hell did that rock come from? It's like someone threw it at Ludlow to knock him over the cliff."

As he whispered those words to himself, he couldn't help but feel a presence close by in the woods. That's when he noticed the smell. It was an awful, pungent odor that seemed to be a combination of rotting flesh and that sulfurous smell that comes from the black, oily mud found in marshes. It burned his nostrils, and his eyes began to water. Whatever made that smell was close. Dangerously close. He turned towards the forest and shone his flashlight into the thick woods. Eye-shine. And those eyes weren't low to the ground like a bear or lion, but six or seven feet higher. And it wasn't the yellow-orange eye-shine animals normally had. It was greenish.

Ben reacted without thinking. He turned his shotgun towards the creature and pulled the trigger. *Blam! Blam! Blam!* Proctor didn't stay around to investigate; he just ran as fast as he could to catch up with the rest of the crew. Time seemed to slow down as he sprinted through the woods then veered back towards the edge of the tree line.

The brain is funny like that. It's almost like a slow-motion camera. It speeds up the input so every minute detail and movement is in perfect focus. He could feel the fear coursing through his veins like ice water, and he felt very much alone. As he cleared the tree line and turned back uphill, he saw the beams from the flashlights up ahead. They had heard the shotgun blasts and stopped.

They saw Ben Proctor's light coming up the mountain towards them. But there was only Proctor's light. Fire fighter Adam Wallace stared at the lone figure making his way up to the lead group. Ludwig was right behind him when they reached the cliff. Wallace hadn't heard anything to indicate Ludwig was in trouble. Where the hell was Ludwig? What the hell was Proctor shooting at?

As Proctor approached the others, he saw everyone staring at him. No one said a word. It was as if they were frozen in disbelief, in anticipation of an explanation for Ludwig's disappearance. The only movement was Captain Robertson making his way down towards Proctor through the statutory line of fire fighters.

"What happened, Ben? Where's Ludwig? What were you shootin' at?"

Proctor just stood there a moment, trying to make sense of what he just witnessed.

"Cap, I don't know exactly what happened. One second, Ludwig was running, and the next... he was gone."

"Gone? What d'ya mean gone? Did he fall or something?"

Robertson could see Proctor was visibly shaken. Something he had never seen in Ben Proctor before.

"No, Cap. He was hit by a huge rock, and it sent him over the edge of that cliff, and he was gone. No noise, no scream, no nothin'. And I'm tellin' you, Cap, somethin' threw that rock. I saw it. Well, I saw its eyes. It was in the woods, and it's pretty big. Maybe seven feet tall, and it *stinks*. We gotta' keep moving. I shot at it, but I didn't stick around to see if I hit it. For all I know, it's still out there."

Robertson could tell there was no use in going back to look for Ludwig. Ben wouldn't have left him out there if he were still alive, and the fire wasn't waiting for them to launch a search and rescue mission. They needed to get to the boulders.

Proctor turned to face down the mountain to see if anything was following them. His imagination placed green-glowing eyes staring at him from the woodland shadows. He stood there, fixated on the darkness below him, numb from the events he just experienced and impervious to his surroundings and the other firefighters behind him. He was trying to make sense of what just happened. Time seemed to stand still. It was like some horror movie was playing out in front of them, only they were to be the victims of some yet to be seen monster. His hypnotic state only lasted a very short seconds, because at that moment, a long, deep, almost moaning howl emanated from the darkened forest below. It lasted almost thirty seconds, but the sound seemed to echo in each fire crew member's mind well after.

Proctor snapped out of his trance. He turned to the others and saw the same fear on their faces that he felt on his own. Before he could say anything, another howl came from the forest above and to the northwest of them. This one was lower, deeper, and resonated with more power than the first, and it was followed by several other howls all around them. As suddenly as they started, they stopped. The only sounds on that mountain were the roar of the fire below and the crackling of burning timber.

The crew was only a few hundred feet from the rock outcrop they were racing towards. Now, it seemed, those rocks might be more than protection from the fire and provide some cover from whatever in these woods was attacking them. No one said a word. They all just turned and began their frantic climb to the rocks.

Captain Robertson reached the rocks first. As he started to turn back to watch the others as they climbed, he felt a light, cool breeze cross the back of his neck. At first, he thought it was a combination of the cold one feels when struck by fear and the shield from the heat that the rocks and boulders offered. Then he noticed a distinct, damp, musty aroma in that breeze. He turned back towards the rocks and strained his eyes to find the source of the breeze. It took him a while to see it. He might have missed it completely had it not been for the smoke. Smoke is very reactive. It moves with very little influence from air movement, which makes the direction of flow easy to track. So when he saw the smoke swirl and move contrary to the prevailing winds at a particular spot, he knew exactly what caused the cool breeze.

"Holy shit! There's a damn cave up here."

If it weren't for the fire, Robertson would never have seen the entrance. It was well camouflaged by several large boulders covering the entrance. He only knew it was there because of the smoke's reaction to the draft from the cave. He knew that caves usually were not a good thing to take advantage of during a fire. Most caves are no more than small holes in the rocks, or shallow caverns just a few feet deep. Death traps. Fires eat oxygen and will suck the breathable air out and fill it with smoke, asphyxiating anything or anyone inside. Cleanup crews have found bears, mountain lions, and numerous small animals lying dead inside caves after a fire burned through, with no signs of burns or injury, suffocated by the lack of air. Robertson knew this cave was different. There was an air flow leaving this cave that was not due to the fire. This draft was almost like a cool breeze leaving the cave, which meant there was probably another point of access which created a draft. If the cave was large enough, it could provide safe cover from the fire for the crew as well as give them cover from whatever made those howls. Robertson shone his flashlight into the cave and saw a short, narrow passage at the beginning that angled down and to the right. As he stood there enjoying the cool, damp, refreshing air that flowed over him, Robertson noticed something besides the musty cave smell on that breeze. There was a hint of decay on that draft. The smell of rotting meat. Probably a bear or lion kill left inside, he thought. He would wait for all the crew to reach the rocks before going farther. Safety in numbers.

It didn't take long for the rest of the crew to reach Robertson's position. It had been an exhausting and adrenaline-charged climb, and the crew was happy to finally be at the rocky outcrop. Instinctively, they started to remove their survival gear and prepared to dig in.

"Hold on, folks. I think there might be an alternative to our original plan." Robertson's voice carried a cheery tone.

"What's up, Cap? Whatcha got?" Proctor was more than happy to hear an alternative plan. Digging in wasn't going to be easy, and it didn't always mean surviving the burn over. At best, it was a fifty-fifty chance.

Robertson stepped back to show everyone the cave entrance.

"I think it goes back pretty deep, and there might be another entrance, because there's a good draft comin' out of here. It should give us pretty good cover from the fire."

It didn't take much convincing to get the crew on board. Their odds of surviving the fire seemed to have gone up.

"I've looked inside with my light, and there seems to be a fairly easy ingress that goes about twenty-five feet or so before heading down to the right. I'll take the lead. Proctor, you continue to bring up the rear. Whatever killed Ludwig might try to follow us in."

Proctor wasn't the type to get nervous. He'd been through and seen a lot in his time in the fire crews. He knew he was the most logical choice for being the rear guard, but that didn't make him feel any more comfortable about it. He couldn't help but feel that nagging sense of being watched, and being at the back left him feeling exposed. Still, he accepted his assignment without question. It was his duty to protect his team from whatever might threaten them. Howling mountain beast be damned.

"Mills. Come in, Mills. Robertson here." Captain Robertson radioed Mills to advise her on their situation and decision to use the cave he'd found.

One by one, each crew member entered the cave. No one noticed the strange symbol that marked this cave as tribal territory etched into the boulder just inside the entrance. Even if they had, they wouldn't have known its significance.

From its position among some dead-falls, the alpha watched the male tribe members scatter across the face of Hoodoo Mountain. The young, wounded male was to get close to the intruders and wait for the last one in line to come by him. He was to remove the offender without being seen. The alpha chose him because he knew he would be limited because of wound. Having only one arm meant it wouldn't be able to pick up larger rocks to throw. Larger rocks or small boulders hurled to the right spots could cause small rockslides that could take out several offenders at once. Not being able to do this relegated it to throwing smaller rocks, basketball sized or so, at one offender at a time. To do this successfully, it would have to be stealthy and attack from behind so as not to be noticed. Eons of tribal experience with this type of tactic had shown the tribe that suddenly losing one human from the group tended to cause the rest of the humans to become disoriented and panicked, making the humans easier to eliminate.

The young male didn't see Proctor bringing up the rear. If it had, it may have survived the attack. When the trespasser passed the juvenile's position, it threw its rock projectile with all the force it could muster. Only after the large rock left its fingers did it see the other human. It tried to recover and find another rock to throw at him, but the trespasser had a thunder stick, and it roared three times, and it was struck by one of the blasts directly in its chest, severing its aorta. It fell back and tried to get to cover before it lost its ability to continue. It fell behind some low shrubs and prepared to die. With its last breath, it let out its death roar. It was long and defiant, and when it was done, so was the juvenile. Twice this night, its lack of experience had caused it to make a costly decision. The second was its final mistake.

The alpha witnessed the juvenile's demise. It can't be said it felt sorrow; not the type felt by humans when one of their own died tragically. It was more like a feeling of the loss of time. The time it takes to sire another tribal member and raise it to an age where it can contribute to the tribe's survival. The time spent raising and training the one that was lost. And, how having one less member would affect tonight's fight. There wasn't much time until sunrise on the Hoodoo, and having one less attacker might affect their ability to totally eliminate the trespassers from their mountain.

The alpha watched the line of lights ascend the mountain as the trespasses fled the fire. It watched as they neared the tribe's lair. There was no time to stop the offenders before they reached the entrance. There it was again. Time. It felt the urgency of time, not as in hours or minutes, but more like a change in the time left on this mountain. The fire was consuming the tribe's lands, the humans were coming to the mountain in ever-increasing numbers and frequency, and they left their own scars on the lands. No respect for the way of the land. No respect for the order of things. And no respect for the tribe.

There was no way the alpha or any member of the tribe could possibly understand that it wasn't a lack of respect for the tribe and its ways. It was simply that so much time had elapsed since humans interacted with the tribe. The old ones, the elders of the human tribes, had died off, leaving fewer and fewer humans knowing the old ways. The younger generation had no patience for learning the old ways. The old ways were too slow, too boring. Silly. What was once tradition, fact, and common knowledge had become folklore, superstition, and fiction. Ghost stories and tales of the boogeyman told around campfires. There was no way the tribe could understand that they were considered nonexistent, not real, fairytale creatures that modern man would be foolish to consider real. Only a handful of tribal elders within the western Native tribes of man kept the traditions and knowledge alive. But even their efforts and ways were looked at by most as hooey. That was not to say others outside Native American tribes didn't believe in the idea of large, hairy, creatures living in the dense forests and swamplands throughout the world. They just didn't know the tribe's ways. They didn't understand what was expected of them when entering tribal territory. Too much time had gone by without meaningful contact between the tribe and humans.

The alpha sat there, watching the trespassers disappear into one of the entrances to its vast cavern lair, and he watched the fire edge ever farther up the mountain. The tribe would deal with these trespassers on their terms, and it would happen inside their home. The cave was where these offenders would spend their last moments. Even if these were the last days of the tribe on this mountain, it would surely be the last moments of life for these offenders. They weren't going anywhere, and they would be easy to contain.

Two of the females would be positioned outside the entrance. They were strong enough to hurl rocks and could call to the males if needed. So the alpha turned his attention towards the other trespassers on their mountain. They were exposed. Even though they would soon reach the more open terrain of the summit, they were still in the thicker, forested northern side of the mountain. The tribe could strike them before they reached the open summit. After they were dealt with, the tribe could then enter their cave from the north entrance and catch the trespassers in the cave and quickly surround them.

He let out a long, bellowing howl that seemed to shake the mountain on all sides. This let the others know to stop where they were. The alpha would direct them with wood knocks and whistles. It was how the tribe had done things from their beginning.

"Holy shit! I ain't never heard anything like that, *ever*."

Stumpy and Team B had just reached Nancy Mills' location when they heard the howl.

"Well, Stumpy, looks like your team's arrival has been announced."

Mills was trying to sound calm and toss out a little humor to break the tension.

"Yeah, well, I ain't too crazy about being on whatever made that noise's radar. People don't seem to fare well once they get noticed."

Stumpy was usually up for shooting one-liners back and forth to keep morale up, but this "howler" had him and the others rattled.

"We better get this damn road opened up to the top as soon as possible. I don't think we're going to be left alone for too long, and I, for one, don't want to be in these thick woods when it comes callin'. It's pretty open at the top, and we'll be better able to see things comin'."

"Well, Stumpy, with your guys here to help, we should be able to punch through this thick crap in a couple hours. We should post some lookouts to try and keep our people safe. How many shotguns do you guys have?"

"Sorry, Nance. Just the one."

Mills had hoped for two, but one was better than none. "Well, let's get our best shots on watch."

Unfortunately, Nancy's best shooter was also her best sawyer. She would have to sacrifice shooting accuracy to keep up the pace clearing the road. After all, how good a shot did one need to be to operate a shotgun at close range? One only needed to get the buckshot somewhere in the zip code for it to be affective. She would take the shotgun and watch over her crew. Seemed like a natural choice. She always seemed to feel like they were her family, anyway. She would find a position where her back was protected and she could see as many of her crew at a time as possible.

Toothless, Yancey, and Hightower had gotten to Mills' position shortly before Stumpy's crew. They had a shotgun, and with Stumpy's, that made three.

"Hey, Toothless, take your shotgun and find a cozy spot below us. Keep anything from sneakin' up on us. Pay attention to our pace up the mountain and move as we do. I don't want to lose track of you. Stumpy, take the flank across from me. I'll try to stay close to the front so I can keep an eye on what's ahead of us. I feel an Excedrin headache comin' on."

"What the hell number Excedrin headache is *monsters in the woods*?"

There was Stumpy's one-liner. Funny thing was, no one laughed. No one laughed, because there were actual monsters in these woods, and they were coming after them. Nothing funny about that.

Everyone was doing their jobs, clearing slash, felling trees, and removing any large rocks that could create problems for the trucks as they moved higher towards the ridge above. Even though Jackson Matoskah was in a bit of a funk, he was doing his job, but his thoughts drifted between the symbol they had seen and his grandfather's campfire stories of a tribe of tall, hairy beasts that lived a solitary life high up in the mountains. Jackson knew he was missing something about those stories. Something important. His grandfather's tales told of members of this tribe and members of the tribes of man having occasional, peaceful contact. There was once an understanding between the tribes. As a child, Jackson only heard the scary parts of the tales. The description of the tribe as being larger than men, covered with hair, sharp teeth, and vengeful in nature, was where young Jackson's focus stayed. Later in life, the tales just seemed like ghost stories to him, something to tell others around the fire but without any truth to them. And yet, there was still that memory of his hunting trip on this very mountain years ago that had left him rattled. Now, as he and the rest of the fire crews faced the mountain and the unseen creature stalking them, he realized there *had* to be some truth in those stories. And in those tales of the tribe were also clues to the ways of the tribe. How to communicate with them. How not to appear as an enemy of the tribe. Clues that could, ultimately, save one's life. Jackson had heard those clues many times but not really listened. So much blah, blah, blah. After all, there couldn't possibly be a tribe of large, hairy creatures living in the mountains. They would have been seen by now. Well, they had been seen, seen by many people, but the sightings were always dismissed as misidentification or made up. Jackson wondered how many of the so-called Bigfoot sightings were in fact sightings of one of the tribesmen.

Jackson's thoughts fell ever deeper, into a trance-like state. His actions were on fully automatic while his thoughts seemed to be guided by some outside force. There were visions of his grandfather and father around the fires of his youth, visions of the tribal elders performing rituals designed to tell the story of the tribe. There was a vision of his grandmother beading his grandfather's possibles bag that he carried whenever he hunted up on the Hoodoo. There was something about the beads. The design. It wasn't the normal bead pattern found on Native American clothing. This was more like a picture. As Jackson's mind focused on his grandfather's quiver, it came into view. It was the same design as the marking carved into the tree. That same strange design. And then it hit him like a two-by-four square in the face. The tales his grandfather had told him were of a way to be safe while traveling in and around the tribe's lands. One had to honor the tribe by branding themselves with the tribe's symbol, the same symbol carved into the tree. If one was entering the tribe's lands, they were to leave an offering of food at the base of one of the marked locations. This was usually a portion of the kill from a hunt. The tribe rarely made contact with the Native American tribes. They would smell the offering and collect it. Whoever left the offering would have left their scent on it. This allowed the tribe to locate the human. They would be able to monitor the human's movements, usually from a distance, and allow the human to pass safely through. Occasionally, a member of the tribe would allow itself to be seen. This was done so that those who traveled in the tribe's lands would know the tribe was there, watching. It was always a fleeting view. They did not stay out of cover for long. Too risky.

Jackson's thoughts raced through this flurry of information as he tried to develop some kind of solution to the events that continued to unfold. He needed to tell Nancy and Stumpy what he knew, and there was no time to lose.

8

HUNTING PARTY

The alpha surveyed the situation before him. Many trespassers had entered his home. His sanctuary. His fortress. And many continued to destroy the tribal lands with their noisy, smelly tools. They would soon reach the middle ridge of their lands. There was easier travel for the trespassers, up there. Years ago, other humans had cut down trees and made a trail for their metal boxes to roll on. They smelled, too. The tribe chose not to do anything to stop the trespassers then. They took some trees and left. The game animals the tribe fed on used that trail to travel, making it easier for the tribe to hunt them. It worked out well for the tribe. As time wore on, more trespassers came to the mountain and took some trees, made new trails, and left. This created more ways for their food to travel easily through the tribal lands. There was more food for the tribe, and the tribe grew. Over time, the trails made by the trespassers became overgrown, narrowing the trails. This made it easy for the tribe to move around their territory without being seen. The trespassers kept some of the trails clear, but many went back to the mountain. The tribe hunted these narrow lanes, and there were many places to ambush their prey. Kills were quick, and few would be left behind; what remained became food for the scavengers.

It seemed that there was no respect for tribal lands, anymore. Trespassers left trash and harvested only part of a kill, leaving a lot of food to go to waste. They even branded the lands with their own symbols, some carved into trees, others left on the rocks. This behavior was what had put the tribe into their current state of mind. Trespassers were not welcome and would be dealt with.

The tribe usually hunted their prey in groups of two to four males. This enabled the tribe to contain its prey and allowed for a quicker kill. It also helped if there happened to be more than one prey animal in the ambush zone. Most kills were performed by hand by breaking the neck of the animal. The shear strength members of the tribe had enabled them to achieve kills in this manner on all but the largest of prey, or if the prey animal was a large predator such as a bear or mountain lion. When encountering one of these, the tribe usually used large rocks to crush the skull. Attempting to grapple with a large predator could injure or kill the hunter, and with the tribes being fairly small in number, a loss of anyone could harm the entire tribe.

These trespassers may not have had sharp teeth or claws, but they carried the thunder sticks. The tribe had seen what kind of damage these sticks could inflict, and the alpha would not risk any more of the members being injured or killed by them. They would attack from the shadows from above the trespassers using large stones, and they would need a lot of them to be successful. As the hunting party moved into position, they would gather stones of the proper size. Each hunter would have a cache of stones to rain death upon the violators. It would not necessarily be a swift death, but the damage to the bodies would render them immobile, and the hunting party could then safely descend into their midst and finish them. It had been done before, and the hunters all knew what to do and what was at stake. The very survival of the tribe hung in the balance. They would not — must not — fail.

This hunting party mentality had served the tribe well. And it was how the tribe would remedy the current trespasser problem. The number of trespassers in the woods was the problem. The tribe only had six males of hunting age and size. There had been seven males, but the earlier loss of the juvenile had left them thin. Females were not allowed to hunt. They were to care for the young and teach them the ways of the tribe. When the males became of age, they would take over the training for the hunt and the hierarchy of the tribe.

Still, there was enough for a hunting party, and the alpha would lead it against the trespassers in the woods. Soon, the trespassers would reach the trail along the crest of the ridge, where the forest was thick on both sides. The hunting party would ambush the trespassers there. Once the alpha knew the direction they would take on that trail, he would set the ambush in motion. There were good spots in either direction. Once these trespassers were punished, the hunters would turn their attention to the ones in the caverns. They weren't going anywhere. The caverns were difficult to navigate, full of dead ends, sudden drop-offs, and many criss-crossing passages. The tribe knew all of these intimately and had the advantage of excellent night vision.

The females would watch the trespassers and, when the time came, would create obstacles for them so the hunting party could easily take them. When the trespassers were no more, the tribe would take the bodies out to the mountain and scatter their remains for the coyotes, bears, and other scavengers to erase. Even the fire that threatened their lands would help erase them from the mountain.

The natural way of things is that everything dies to help the living. Plants die and fertilize the soil so other plants can grow. Animals die and their carcasses feed the carnivores and birds. It had always been and always would be this way.

The tribe would now be silent. They would not betray their positions or their movements, so they could move to corral the trespassers. The alpha would watch the trespassers himself. He could not afford another mistake by a younger, less experienced member. He would ensure his tribe would survive and those who chose to desecrate their lands would not. The fire raging over the lands was the only unknown. He needed to watch the fire as well. They would burn in fire, like everything else. Even if the trespassers were destroyed, the fire could destroy them. The continuation of the tribe was the most important thing to the alpha, even above punishing the trespassers. The trespassers had to honor the tribe, but the tribe had to honor the fire.

Time. That is the enemy above all enemies. No matter the culture, species, or way of life. Time never stops to ponder the situation. Time never pauses for opportunity to catch up. Time always wins in the end.

Soon, the light of day would creep into the mix. This would hinder the tribe's ability to stay hidden. The shadows would be erased. Soon, the trespassers would reach the upper trail and be able to move a little faster, maybe fast enough to get past the ambush spot before the tribe could position themselves. Soon, the fire would be upon them, and the tribe would have to seek the shelter of the caverns. There might be too many enemies for the tribe to fight. Trespassers, fire, and time. Even if the tribe was to vanquish these trespassers, would their time on this mountain be over? Would they, too, be relegated to mere ghost stories of the past, haunting the shadows of men's minds, kept alive only through the stories told by the elders of the local Native tribes? Even those stories could be lost to time as they were told less and less as elders lost their battles with time. Time always wins. It's just a matter of time. And time was running out for all on Hoodoo Mountain.

"Hey, Nance, I think I've figured something out. I know it's going to sound crazy, but just hear me out." Jackson Matoskah was out of breath from running down to Mills' location. It wasn't that far a trip, but the smoke made it hard to breathe.

Mills barely even looked in Jackson's direction. Her eyes were fixed on the shadows, searching the darkness for any sign of movement and hoping the orange glow from the fire would give her a glimpse of whatever was tormenting the crews. She wanted to see for herself what Anderson, Davidson, and Jeffries had encountered, to see what kind of animal could wreak so much havoc on the crews and heavy equipment, to see for herself if this could be the work of some kind of unknown creature. She peered intently into the night, watching the shadows shift in the flickering glow. The fire gave the shadows a life of their own, and she wouldn't take her eyes off of them for fear that at any minute there would be something there. Something hidden in the shadows until revealed by the firelight. She couldn't take the chance on missing an opportunity to take her at it. She couldn't let any more of her crew be hurt or worse. They were family.

Nancy heard Jackson talking to her, but the words weren't registering.

"Nance, did you hear what I said?" Matoskah repeated.

"I think I have something, Nance. Might be important."

The urgency in Matoskah's voice snapped Mills out of her daze.

"Sorry, Jack. What ya' got?"

Matoskah knew his information might sound nuts but didn't have a choice.

"I know what I'm going to say might sound crazy. But just hear me out."

Matoskah let it all out. The tribal tales of the Seatco, the legend of the tribe and how they were known as the guardians in the woods. He explained how his grandfather carried the symbol of the tribe sewn onto his quiver, the same symbol they had seen on a tree earlier, and how it seemed to offer protection to those who bore it, how the symbol marked those as understanding and respecting the ways of the tribe and their lands.

"What the hell are you tellin' me, Jack? If we paint our faces, we walk out of here? What kind of bullshit is that?"

"Sorry, Jack. I guess this whole situation has me wired tighter than hell. But you have to admit, this sounds pretty far-fetched. People actually communicating with Bigfoot? Is that what you're tellin' me? Your people actually believe there's a fuckin' tribe of bigfoots up here, and they have *rules*? I just don't know what to say about all that."

"I told you it was going to sound crazy, Nance. I can hardly get my head wrapped around it either. But my people believe it, my grandfather believed it, and, to be perfectly honest, I'm starting to believe it too. It all adds up. The damage to our gear, the attacks. I think this tribe of Seatcos thinks we are destroying their mountain. Think about it. First, some stupid kids set their woods on fire with some fireworks. We know at least one of those kids is dead. We found his bloody wallet. Then we show up and start cutting trees, axing bushes, and starting backfires. There's no way they could know we are here to help. How could they?"

Mills looked into Matoskah's eyes.

"You're serious, aren't you?" Mills could tell by Jackson's tone. She knew he wasn't prone to fantastic stories. Matoskah was always level-headed.

"Yes. I know how it sounds, but you tell me. What else could it be? A bear? They don't travel in packs and throw rocks. A band of crazy people? They would have to be awfully big and strong crazy people. It's the only thing that fits."

"Well, you've got a point on the whole bears and crazy people thing. But a tribe of sasquatches... C'mon, Jack. You have to admit, it sounds more than a little bizarre."

Mills was trying hard to convince herself that there was some other explanation, but deep down, she knew Jack's explanation made sense. She didn't have a lot of time to mull it over. Call it women's intuition, ESP, or just extreme situational awareness, but she had a bad feeling things would get ugly if they continued with the same course of action. That damn definition of insane, doing the same thing and expecting different results, kept rolling through her mind.

"Okay, Jack. What do you have in mind?"

"Well, Nance. I say we take a page from my people's playbook. I need a Sharpie."

There was a logbook in the cab of every truck. The pages were made of a special type of material that could withstand the rigors of backwoods firefighting. The only writing instrument that would work on it was a Sharpie. It had the added benefits of being quick to dry and permanent, a real plus if it was dowsed with water or the liquid fire retardant the aerial assault crews used. Matoskah wasted no time in retrieving one from the closest truck.

"Let me have your hard hat, Nance."

Jack quickly recreated the symbol they had seen carved into the rocks and trees, the same symbol beaded onto his grandfather's hunting quiver. He drew it on both sides of the hard hat, since the front and back had his name and assigned number. He then did the same to all the hard hats. As he did, he felt a strange oneness with his ancient heritage. A newfound feeling of pride in his people and their history, as if his grandfather's spirit was there with him as he emblazoned the symbol of the Seatco on official government property. He couldn't help but laugh at the thought of what the division commanders would say when they saw it. Assuming, of course, they lived to return to base. Matoskah got his fair share of ribbing from the rest of the crew; it was to be expected. After all, these were mostly veteran fire crews. Even the most junior on the crew were experienced woodsman, hunters, and outdoorsman, none of whom had ever come across anything like what Matoskah was talking about. At least, not until this trip. The only one that didn't say anything to him was Mark Anderson. Matoskah had gone over his grandfather's story of the creature he had encountered while building a fire tower up on Scotchman's Peak, so many years ago. It rekindled the spine-tingling fear he'd had as a kid when first hearing the story. In Anderson's mind, Matoskah's explanation was just as good as any. Maybe better.

Lastly, Jack would put the emblem on the truck doors. They would be larger and easier to see from a distance.

While working on one of the trucks, the radio crackled to life. It had been quiet for some time and startled Matoskah.

"Fire base command to forward fire crew, Hoodoo. Come in, Hoodoo! Over."

Fire base command was in Coeur d'Alene, Idaho. It was the relay station for all fire operations in Northern Idaho, as it was the least likely location to lose power or have sketchy radio service. They could co-ordinate all aspects of fire suppression efforts from multiple locations.

"Hey, Stumpy! Command's calling you on the horn," Matoskah hollered.

Matoskah signed off while Stumpy ran to the truck to answer. "Roger, command... Forward fire Hoodoo team leader, Stumpy here. Go ahead. Over."

"Stumpy, I know things have been rough on you guys up there. We've been trying to reach Captain Robertson or anyone from alpha team, but they are not answering. What's going on up there?"

"Their signal is probably blocked, sir. They had to take shelter in a cave system. Fire almost overtook them. They've lost Ludwig."

"Sorry to hear that, Stumpy. Did the fire get him? What happened?"

Up to this point, no one had officially notified base operations of attacks or what might be doing them. It had all been radio chatter and vague allegations of animal, or possible human, interference with the fire crews. Stumpy felt it was time to let fire base command know what had been happening. He would stop short of saying Bigfoot.

"No, command. We've encountered something or someone that's attacking our crews. We're not exactly sure what we're dealing with. Haven't been able to get any good looks at whatever it is. All we know is there seems to be more than one, and we've lost some men and equipment. We have armed ourselves and are continuing to move to the upper fire service road at the peak. We hope to swing back through the burn area and locate alpha team once we have established our fore lines and back-burns."

"What the hell are you talking about, Stumpy? Who in their right mind would be up on that mountain now? It doesn't make sense. You sure of what you're saying, Sam?"

Stumpy knew exactly how this sounded and needed to tread a fine line here.

"Ten-four, command. That's all we've got so far."

Stumpy wasn't going to put his career on the line over an unproven theory.

"Roger that, Stumpy. Keep us updated. I may have some good news for you and your crew. We have a break in the weather coming. Winds should calm down enough for some air support by midmorning. Hang in there and be ready to co-ordinate the drops. Over."

"Ten-four, command. That's great news. We should be at the upper fire service road before then. Out."

Stumpy quickly got the word out that aerial water drops may be coming in just a few hours. With that good news, everyone seemed rejuvenated, and a new sense of urgency to reach the upper road before daybreak had replaced the stifling fear. Oh, the fear was still there — just pushed to the back of their minds. Some of the crew felt a little ridiculous having the new symbol on their hard hats, but others felt it might actually help protect them. Only time would prove which was correct.

"Command said they've been trying to reach the captain but didn't have any luck. You think they're okay, Nance?"

Stumpy had had a bad feeling about them entering the caves right from the beginning. No communication meant there was no way to get updates, co-ordinate efforts, or even get help to them. Add to the mix that they were still being pursued by whatever was out there, it was nothing but bad news.

"I'm sure they're good, Stumpy. Those guys are probably laughing at us out here in the heat of the fire. They're probably enjoying the cool temps in the cave. Hell, I bet there's water in there, and they've all taken a bath and are smellin' all pretty while we stink up the place. Don't worry, Sam. Those guys know what they're doing."

"You're probably right. I just don't like not having any contact."

"I'm sure we'll hear from them just as soon as the fire clears their location. As fast as that fire is moving up that draw, probably only be a half hour or so."

Mills was doing her best to calm her own fears. Call it woman's intuition. Call it experience. Or call it just a gut feeling. She had the same concerns as Stumpy. Only her concerns went beyond the obvious professional ones. She had a personal interest in one person in particular. She hoped Ben was safe. She found herself wanting to cry but suppressed that almost as soon as that emotion came over her. Can't have a team leader getting all soft and mushy. How would that look to her crew? They would see it as a sign of weakness. It is the ever-present conundrum faced by all women in leadership positions. How to be strong, resilient, and decisive without appearing to be a heartless, headstrong, ball-busting bitch. Mills had mastered the balancing act. Her crew respected her. They trusted her judgement. They had almost forgotten that she was, in fact, a woman. To them, she was their leader and a valued member of the crew. This may have been one reason Ben Proctor hadn't approached her as a woman. Maybe it was time for her to show him her softer side. That would have to wait. For now, it was all about survival and doing their jobs. She said a silent prayer for him and all the crew's safety.

9

BREAK

There was something in the wind. He could smell it. Taste it. A change was coming in the weather. They were very attuned to their surroundings. They had to be. Subtle changes in weather patterns affected their game and how they hunted them. Before a storm, their prey would go on a feeding frenzy, gorging themselves so they could weather the storm without fear of hunger. Bad weather obscured the smell of predators. Wind and rain masked sounds and made it difficult to hear danger. So prey animals would typically bed down until the weather changed. They would go back out to forage for food when they could once again be aware of predators.

These behavioral patterns dictated how and when the tribe hunted. After all, hunting expended energy reserves. An unsuccessful hunt meant not replenishing those reserves. Oh, there were alternatives to meat. But vegetation doesn't offer the same fuel as protein. It takes a lot of protein to power seven- to nine-foot, 800-pound mammals. It is one reason this tribe chose this mountain as their home. There was plenty of game, and there had always been humans living close to the base of the mountain.

Humans grew all manner of food. The vegetables were higher in nutrients than the wild greens, and there were always easily accessible proteins in numbers that could usually augment the tribe's diet without drawing too much attention to their existence. When normal prey animals were scarce due to environmental factors such as fire, drought, or migratory reasons, the tribe could rely on those food sources to carry them. They would have to be careful not to overfeed on those sources. Too many kills draws too much attention, and they could not risk being found. And the risks had multiplied.

Humans had developed new technologies to aide them in predator identification and the locating game animals. Game cameras — the tribe did not know them as this. They only know that some of the trees where humans go have small boxes that flash a bright, white light that interferes with their night vision. Others don't flash but have a high-pitched sound that is almost undetectable to all but the most sensitive ears. These cameras don't capture too many images of tribe members, as the high-pitched tone can be heard by the tribe long before they are in range of the device. When they hear the sound, they simply alter their course to avoid them. They don't understand their purpose; they just know to avoid them so they don't hurt their ears. Still, it is a risk to their anonymity and must be avoided. If found, they will destroy them if they can do so without being discovered. Many are destroyed each year, and most humans are none the wiser that it was the tribe. They attribute the losses to thieves or bears. Occasionally, though, a tribe member is photographed on one of these devices. Fortunately for the tribe, their ability to stay hidden has led to modern day humans believing those photos to be hoaxes or misidentification.

The attacks on the trespassers had expended a lot of energy, and they needed to eat. The fire had chased off most of the larger food sources, and the smaller animals took too much energy to catch. They would need to send a forager down to the valley to gather food. The alpha would normally go, but he was needed on the mountain. Instead, a younger but strong subordinate would be sent. He had to go and return before daylight. The alpha had shown those of age where to go and what paths to take to avoid human contact. It should be a relatively quick and simple task. The alpha instructed a young male to go and gather the food. This was considered an honor, for lack of a better term. The tribe did not use such terminology. It was understood that if one was asked to perform such a task, it was known to all the tribe that that member had been elevated above being a mere member. That one may very well be a future alpha and was to be respected.

While the young male made his way down the mountain, the alpha watched the trespassers. And he watched the skies. There was a change in the weather. He could feel the wind change in force, and it was coming from a different direction. Maybe they wouldn't have to fight the trespassers *and* the fire. Maybe the fire would move. Maybe the fire would die. He had seen fire die before on this mountain. There were parts of the mountain that wouldn't burn. The top of the mountain had a large area where there were few trees and many large boulders.

Some of those boulders had hollow places from which to attack without being in the way of the thunder sticks. The tribe had been storing large rocks in and around those boulders for years. They had done this in many other locations all over the mountain. By having these rocks in place ahead of time, they were able to hunt only for food and not weapons. This conserved energy and allowed the tribe to move from ambush location to ambush location without having to carry any rocks. This made them much faster and resulted in a higher success rate for hunting. It would also help them in their ambush on the trespassers. It would be devastating. For now, they waited for the alpha to signal for them to attack.

The young male made his way down the mountain and across the gravel roads to the area he would go gather food from. He had been there before with the alpha. It had been some time, and things were somewhat different, but the way was still clear in his mind. He would follow the game trail that twisted below the area where the humans lived. From the trail, he could make short probes up the hill to seek easy food sources. He could smell the chickens, goats, and pigs as he made his way through the area. He stopped and watched the woods for a while to make sure the path was clear. He would follow a narrow game trail up the hill to where he could smell the food. All was quiet, and there were no humans in sight. He proceeded up the hill without a sound, when a bright flash blinded him for a moment. Then there was another flash and another.

He ran up the trail and veered off to the side of it to allow his eyes to re-adjust to the darkness. He stood there, listening for anything that could be a threat. All was quiet. There was nothing but the sounds of the woods and the smells from the food. When his night vision returned, he saw where the flash had come from. It was one of those boxes on a tree. He became enraged, tore the box from the tree, and threw it down the hill. Then he returned to the task at hand. Food.

There, in a small pen, he saw his target. A large, fat pig. It was enough food to feed the tribe for a couple of days. He knew this animal made loud noises when attacked. The kill would have to be swift, and the prey would need to be unaware of his presence. He also knew that he would have to crush this animal's skull to kill it. Its neck was too thick to quickly break. The first time he had come upon this type of food, he was being trained in the ways of the hunt. He had tried to break the neck of that one, but the animal put up a violent fight to survive, all the while squeezing and snorting and gnashing its teeth. He had almost lost his grip on the animal before the older male smashed the pig's head in with a large rock. The noise that animal made woke up the humans, and they were almost found out. They were lucky to slip into the dark woods with their food in hand, uninjured and undiscovered. Lesson learned. He needed a large rock.

He checked the wind and quietly approached with it blowing in his face. Once he knew the animal was not aware of him being there, he struck. No noise. No struggle. A clean kill. The pig weighed over 400 pounds. The young male put the pig under one arm and headed back to Hoodoo Mountain and the tribe. He would take it back to the females of the tribe to be portioned out. The time for the ambush of the trespassers was quickly arriving, and there wasn't enough time for him to do the chore and return to his place. He could not use the closest cavern entrance as it was where the other trespassers had entered. He would not be able to deliver the meal to the females without being seen, so he would need to use an entrance higher up the mountain. This was not as desirable as it was farther from the central cavern area where the females and very young were. It would take more time. Time... It never stops and never waits for anyone or anything. He would need to move quickly.

From his perch high atop a thinly wooded, rocky crag, the alpha could see the movement of the trespassers without being seen. There was little risk of that at this time, due to the humans' poor vision in the dark. Still, the humans did have the ability to pierce the dark with beams of light. With that, they might be able to catch sight of him, so he would stay low and sit still. He didn't need to see everything; they had a heightened sense of smell, just like all natural beings that lived in the wilderness. Humans had once had that, but most had lost it or left it undeveloped; now, they could only smell the most pungent of odors.

Unfortunately, the tribe members carry a very strong odor. Each tribe has their own unique scent, which helps them identify its members or even rival tribes on their lands. It also aids them in the hunt. To be successful, they need to keep their scent away from their prey and, even though humans had a less developed sense of smell, they would use the same tactics as when hunting food.

As the alpha took in all the sights and smells of the mountain, he caught the scent of the forager he had sent. If these creatures were capable of smiling, the alpha would have done so at the recognition of the smell of the food it brought back. This type of food animal was unique, as almost all of it was edible. What little hair was on these animals was easily spit out. The tribe was less concerned with the taste of their food. It was nutrition, a way to replenish energy stores. Taste rarely dictated what they hunted. But this food animal had the added benefit of tasting good. A fitting meal for his tribe as they defended their lands. They would eat after dealing with these trespassers. Then, already being in the caverns where the others had gone, they would eliminate that threat to them. After that, they would simply wait for the fire to pass.

Hopefully, their lands would still be habitable after the burn. If not, they were prepared to move. But they most likely would not have to move, as the mountain had many suitable places to hunt and forage. Fire had visited this mountain before, and the tribe had been there. In the memories carried by the tribe, they had always been there and would always be there. The caverns never changed, and there was always water flowing into the system. They would be able to stay in the caves and, if need be, simply hunt and forage in a different part of the mountain. For now, the fire was not as big a threat to the tribe as the humans were. Not just these trespassers, but the others that would surely come once the fire was gone.

Fire renews life on the mountain in the form of fresh growth of many varieties of trees, shrubs, berries, and mushrooms. Humans came to the mountain after fires to forage for the bountiful growth of morel mushrooms, a staple for the tribe and a delicacy for the humans. The tribe knew to leave some for future harvests, but the humans took all they could see. Fire opened the spores left behind to furtive soils, and the right amount of sun spurred an explosion of growth. The humans knew this, so the tribe would gather only those in the most inaccessible areas. Fire leaves ashes, ashes make for soft ground, and soft ground makes a great medium for clear footprints. Footprints that could lead humans to the tribe's whereabouts. Leaving footprints in the soil was an inevitable fact in the lives of all creatures in the wilderness. But all creatures try not to leave too detailed a trail to be followed. Hopefully, any tracks would be erased or made indistinguishable by rain, wind, or other natural forces before being detected by those who would follow. All these things the alpha had to consider at all times. It was the alpha's responsibility to do so and protect his group — his family, as it were. For now, his focus was on the upcoming tasks. How the alpha chose to handle the attack and when could determine whether or not the tribe had a future on these lands or even a future at all.

10

THE CAVERN

They could smell them when they entered their lair. They smelled of sweat, fear, and smoke. The tribe's keen sense of smell could separate many different odors that other creatures emitted. They could distinguish whether what they were smelling was male or female, sick or healthy, and even calm or frightened. This innate ability enabled the tribe to determine if what they were smelling was a threat or not and, during a hunt, if their prey was alert to their presence or not. Knowing if their prey was healthy or sick could determine if they even wanted to take it for food. Some diseases could be detrimental to the tribe, while others just made the prey weaker and less likely to put up much of a fight. Good information to have, especially when dealing with threats. The strength and numbers of a threat would determine the tribe's tactics in dealing with it.

The preservation of the tribe was of the highest priority. The young were the future, and there would be no young without healthy females and at least one or two breeding males. For this reason, during times of natural and unnatural threats, the alpha would have the females and younger members stay within the relative safety of the caverns. There were many chambers to hide in and a maze of ways to reach those chambers. Some paths in the cavern led to dead ends, some to entrance or exit points, and others to bedding sites and food caches.

This threat to the tribe was now within their very home. The alpha had charged the adult females to observe and contain the trespassers, avoiding contact, if possible, until the alpha and other males returned from dealing with the trespassers outside the cavern. The advantage was definitely with the tribe. Home field advantage, so to speak. The cavern was dark. They could see in the dark. The cavern was difficult to navigate. They knew the cavern intimately. They had superior numbers, and they were much larger than the trespassers.

The only advantage to the trespassers was their thunder sticks. And that was a huge problem for the tribe. They had already lost a member to the thunder sticks, and the trespassers in the cavern had two. They could even smell the metal and the acrid gunpowder. They might not have known what those odors were, but they knew it meant danger. They had witnessed many humans in the past use different thunder sticks to kill deer, elk, and many other prey animals. Some from very long distances. They didn't know how they worked, and they didn't know there were limits on how many times a thunder stick could boom, but they knew to stay away from the hollow end.

For now, they would position themselves at various places inside the cavern, where they could keep track of the trespassers' movements by the strength of their scent. There were many natural vents in the cavern. These kept the air from getting stale. They also flowed from specific areas within the cavern. The strength of the scent from a particular vent would determine where the trespassers were in the cavern. The beta female was given the task of keeping the trespassers in view. She could relay any information regarding the movements before their scent traveled through the vents.

Outside, wood knocks were part of their communication. In the cavern, rock knocks traveled better, and the sound could be considered natural to the untrained ear. The "language" of knocking was not very detailed — usually only one to three knocks in succession with pauses of varying lengths between any further knocking. It was the time between the knocks that indicated urgency or not. Shorter time, more urgent. Longer time, less urgent. Basic, simple, yet hard to discern for outsiders. Knocks also kept the tribe members from vocalizing. Without vocalizations, it was hard to determine if a noise came from a living creature or was just a natural sound in nature. They knew exactly where the trespassers were, how many of them there were, and if they were moving or staying put. They also knew the trespassers were scared. Sweat gives off a sickly-sweet smell when fear sets off the fight-or-flight adrenaline rush. And that smell permeated the cavern.

The fire raged just outside the cavern entrance. Captain Robertson and what remained of Team A's fire crew huddled together at the end of the narrow corridor that led to a larger, room-like cave. Between sending crew members to Mills' location and the loss of George Ludlow, they were down to five. Not a comfortable number considering the situation.

The ceiling of the cave was no more than seven feet for as far as they could see but maybe over a hundred feet wide, and the floor slanted downward at a comfortable angle for walking and looked to be about fifty feet deep. After that, all they could see was black. They would do a more involved reconnoiter after they took full inventory of their situation. But, for lack of a better term, they were comfortable for the time being; the fire crew was thankful to be alive, especially under the strange circumstances they found themselves immersed in. Not only did it seem the fire was trying to kill them, but they also had to deal with an unidentified creature bent on killing them. For now, they were thankful for the coolness of the cavern.

"Okay, ladies. Let's get our heads in the game."

Captain Robertson knew he needed to rally the team and refocus their energy. These were experienced, well-trained men. To a man, they were fearless in the face of danger. But they were human, after all, and humans have vast imaginations when it comes to the unknown or unexplained. This could lead some to fall into an almost paralyzed mental state. Training usually took over when it came to the tasks at hand. Training and retraining leads to muscle memory and an almost automatic reaction to the variables one may encounter while fighting fires. There was no training for what they had just been through. There was no muscle memory or automatic reaction. This was unexplored territory, and Robertson was making it up as he went, relying on basic survival training to address this threat.

"Let's get a tally on supplies." His voice was calm but firm. The tone reassured the battle-weary firefighters, and they felt an uneasy but somewhat relaxed focus on the task at hand.

"Let's start with water. How many canteens, and how much in each? Squatch?"

Ben Proctor was usually good at conserving water, and this time was no exception.

"I've got three canteens, Cap. Grabbed a couple extra off the truck just before it headed up to Mills. Figured they would have the water tank on the truck, and they could refill their canteens. Two are full, and one is half full."

Proctor was always thinking, keeping his head in the game and planning for any variable. It was one of the things that made him a good team leader.

"Smart thinking, Squatch. That'll help a bit. Peterson?"

"I got one canteen about half full, Cap."

"Dutch, how about you?"

"I have two canteens. One's about three quarters empty, but Matthews gave me his before he left, and that one's still full."

"And Wallace, how about you?"

Wallace had already checked his water and was glad there were a few extra canteens. Somewhere along the way, his canteen had gotten a small hole poked and drained dry.

"Sorry, Cap. Damn thing's got a hole in it and it's empty."

The fire-retardant clothing the crews wore was so sturdy, Wallace didn't even notice the leak, even though it had dripped all down the back of his pants. Even if he could have felt the dampness from the leak, it was likely the stress of the situation would have blocked him from noticing until such a time like now, when everything seemed to calm down from the harrowing moments of just a few minutes earlier. The remaining crew had yet to fully deal with the horrifying death of George Ludlow.

"Don't sweat it, Wallace. Looks like we're covered on water and, by the smell off this cave, there may be water in deeper." Robertson felt good about the water but would still ration what they had until they could get more.

"Does anyone have any purification tabs? Just in case we find water in here, I don't want anyone getting the squirts."

"I've got a full pack, Cap. Enough for the canteens we've got." Proctor was famous for raiding the supply cabinet before any fire suppression mission.

"Geez, Squatch, what'd ya do, horde all the med supplies?" Joked Dutch.

"You'll be glad I got the damn tabs, Dutch. Who knows what critters have been peeing in the water in this cave."

"You know, Squatch, it does kinda smell like somethin's been pissing in this cave."

Dutch was right. There was a smell of urine mixed with the dank smell from the caverns and the smell of smoke that seemed to cling to everyone.

Captain Robertson wanted to finish the inventory of supplies.

"Okay, okay. We have two shotguns. How many shells do we have? I've got half a box. Squatch?"

"Almost half a box, Cap. I reloaded after shootin' at that... whatever it was that killed Ludlow."

That brought everyone back into focus. What was it that killed Ludlow, and were there more? There almost certainly were more. After all, they had heard the howls that seemingly echoed all around them right after Proctor shot that thing. Now they were wondering, were there any of those things in here? A sudden surge of fear pulsed through all the men's veins. A collective chill filled the air and, almost to a man, that strange, sinking, pit-of-the-stomach feeling set in.

"Get a grip, guys. We've got plenty of ammo. We're okay on water. That fire's gonna burn too hot for us to leave the way we came in for at least the next few hours. Let's settle in for thirty minutes and catch our breath. Then we oughta look at seeing where this cave goes. Might be a way out. That breeze keeping the smoke out has gotta come from somewhere."

Robertson was relieved that they were in pretty good shape with supplies and no one was injured. They might just make it out of this thing in one piece. As long as there weren't any more incidents with those "things."

She crept in closer for a better look at the intruders. She knew this cavern so well, she knew exactly where she could step without making any noise. Couple that with the ability to see in total darkness, and she could maneuver extremely close without being seen. What she felt wasn't really anger for the intruders. They were not susceptible to the types of emotions humans felt. What they felt was more of a right and wrong, or survive or die feeling. Intruders threatened the tribe's survival, so it was right to defend their lands. Killing wasn't done out of hatred, and there was no joy in it other than knowing the tribe would go on.

There is nothing more basic than the feeling of accomplishment upon surviving. Ask most any human that has survived insurmountable odds, and they will say it's a feeling almost impossible to describe. Euphoria seems to be the closet description. Humans have the survivors' club, people who lived through events who never should have. The tribe had no such club. They had the tribe itself. And as long as the tribe survived, that was all that mattered in their struggle to remain.

As much as this sentry wanted to attack the small group of intruders, she would not. It was her duty to the tribe to watch, for now. An involuntary, almost imperceptible, guttural growl emanated from her. It wasn't intentional and was barely audible, but the cavern's walls acted like a sounding board, and it seemed like a howl in her mind. She would hold still to keep the intruders from seeing her.

"Did you hear that, Cap? Sounded like a bear growling or something." Roger Pederson was always hearing things the rest of the crew couldn't. It was uncanny. Once, when he and the rest of Team A was fighting a fire in Bonner's Ferry, he kept saying, "I hear a chopper. I swear there's a water chopper coming in." Everyone had said he was crazy. He was hearing things. But, sure enough, a few minutes went by, and then everyone heard the unmistakable sound of a helicopter flying in to drop water on the fire. Ever since, no one doubted his ears.

"A bear? Great! That's just what we need to add to the mix."

Wallace voiced what the others were thinking. What else would they have to deal with on this fire? Fire, high winds, multiple deaths of fellow crew members... monsters. And now... a fucking bear.

"Didn't hear it, Wallace. But we all know your bionic ears. Where'd it come from?" Robertson moved up by Wallace and turned his headlamp on.

"Sounded like it was down there, deeper in the cave."

Robertson shone his light into the darkness, slowly moving it left to right. If there was a bear, either its eye-shine would give it away, or it might move in reaction to the light. He moved slowly from one side to the other, making sure to study every shadow and boulder for signs of a bear. Nothing.

"Could've been the wind moving through the cavern. It can make all kinds of weird noises."

Wallace wasn't so sure. He would keep his eyes on the darkened cavern below for signs of anything lurking in the shadows.

"Maybe, Cap. But I'm gonna keep watching. Just in case."

Her white hair blended perfectly with the gray and other light-colored rocks in the cavern. For the moment, she had gone unseen, but Pederson wouldn't let it go.

"Give it a rest, Pederson. You're lettin' your nerves get to ya'."

Dutchauser was edgy. He didn't like caves much, and all Pederson's talk of growls was making him more uncomfortable. He hoped he could keep his nervousness hidden from the others by telling Pederson to calm down when it was actually his own nerves he needed to calm.

Everyone was on alert. All eyes and ears were straining to hear or see something, all the while they hoped they wouldn't.

She wasn't the only tribe member closing in on the fire crew. Three others had maneuvered into different positions so not to allow the trespassers to escape. The fire raging outside the cavern would keep them from leaving the way they came in. The four tribe members would keep them here until the males arrived.

The only chink in their armor that could expose them were their eyes. Their eyes were so adapted to the dark that they had eye-shine even with little or no ambient light to reflect. This meant they needed to keep from looking directly at the intruders. If they happened to be looking directly at them when even the slightest of light struck them, their eyes would give off a bright green reflection and give away their locations. For this reason, they tended to keep their heads tilted down so their eyes would be somewhat concealed by their long hair as it draped down over their eyes. But even this didn't guarantee their eyes wouldn't reflect.

Just as one of the females was settling into her vantage point, one of the trespassers shined a light up into the cavern, striking her directly in the face. She instinctively closed her eyes and froze.

"Holy shit! Did you guys see that? I saw green eye-shine. Something's in here with us."

Pederson had turned on his flashlight at just the right moment to catch the eyes of one of the tribe's females. He hadn't seen the whole figure of the creature; it was too deep in the cavern, but he had definitely seen the eyes of the beast.

"I fuckin' told you I heard something. I fuckin' told you."

There would be no doubt Pederson was right. Captain Robertson had seen it too. And so had Dutchauser.

"Everyone, just calm down. We have two shotguns and plenty of ammo. It's probably a bear or cougar who's just as scared as we are trying to get away from the fire. Let's just keep an eye on that spot and see what happens."

Robertson wasn't sure about the bear and cougar thing. They don't have green eye-shine. As a matter of fact, he didn't recall ever seeing any animal with green eye-shine.

"Hey, Squatch, shine your light up there and see if you can get a bead on what's up there."

Proctor aimed his light towards where they had seen the eye-shine. Eyes can play funny tricks on a person. While looking for one thing, they might not even notice something else. A person might even misidentify something because of a preconceived idea. Once, while deer hunting from a tree stand, he had seen two grouse hunters and their black lab cross over a small ridge. A few minutes later, he saw that black lab running along the deer trail he was watching. He first saw the dog about 600 yards away and had thought, *That dog is running kinda funny.* He watched as the dog approached, and it wasn't until it had gotten within fifty yards of him that he noticed it wasn't a dog at all. It was a black bear. It must've been spooked by those grouse hunters. Because he had seen the black lab, Proctor's brain went into auto pilot and misidentified the bear. So it was understandable that when his light shined right on the female tribe member, he didn't notice it right away. After all, he wasn't looking for a Seatco. He was looking for a bear or a cougar. Still, as he moved the light off her and along the boulders that littered the cavern, his brain had noticed that one of those boulders looked kind of hairy. When that thought registered in, Proctor immediately turned the light back towards the "hairy rock." It moved only slightly, but it *moved*. An icy cold rushed throughout his entire body. Whatever killed Ludlow was right here in this cave. But how could that be? He had shot the damn thing. They had all heard its death moans. They had also all heard howls of many others all around them. He was certain now. There were more of these creatures. *Lots* more.

The movement of the creature was slight. He wasn't sure if anyone else had seen it and didn't want to cause a panic. He started to turn to let Robertson know what he had seen, when he caught a glimpse of another "hairy rock." There were *two* of those things in here with them. Two that he knew of. What if there were more? He leaned in close to Captain Robertson and was going to whisper what he had seen, but Robertson already knew. He had seen the movement too. It was time to formulate a defensive plan. The advantage was definitely with these creatures. They were big, strong, and could see in the dark. There was no telling how many more of these things were in there with them. What he knew was they were trapped. No radio signal was getting out of the cavern — no way to call for help. They were on their own.

Robertson turned to face the crew. He knew they were in a life and death situation, and he knew it was possible — hell, even probable — that this cavern would be where they would meet their ends.

"Men, I don't know if you all saw what Squatch and I just saw up there in those boulders, so here it is. Looks like there are more of those things that killed Ludlow and may have killed Moore. There are at least two of 'em right here in this cavern. There may be more. They haven't attacked yet, but they might. Let's get ourselves set, just in case. We know there's probably none behind us because of the fire, so let's stay focused on our front and our flanks. Squatch and I will take up shooting positions. Pederson, you watch our left. Dutch, take the right. Wallace, you take charge of the ammo and get it to us fast if we need it. Everyone know what to do?"

Everyone acknowledged their assignments and deftly got into position. Theirs would be a strictly defensive position. No shots would be fired unless they were attacked.

The eldest female studied the movements of the trespassers below. She sensed that they were aware of the tribe's presence. It was not her role to attack these intruders, but she could let them know there was no way out. She let out a long and guttural howl that was quickly echoed by the six others hidden within the caverns. Their howls rocked the walls of the caves. The shape of the walls and ceiling reverberated their howls so that they seemed to be coming from every direction. This went on for several minutes and, as if on cue, suddenly stopped. The echoes of the howls could be heard for a few more seconds as they traveled deep into the tribe's lair. And then, there was silence. Dead silence.

The fire crew could hear their own hearts beating, and a paralyzing fear swept over them. All they could do was watch and wait. They weren't trained for this. They were firefighters, not soldiers.

How in the hell could anyone train for this type of situation, anyway? Where does someone go to learn defensive strategies while engaged with multiple bigfoots? That's when the irony of the situation hit Proctor. They had survived the fire, so far, but were probably going to be killed by a creature that supposedly didn't exist. In fact, Bigfoot had become somewhat of a novelty all over the country. There were Bigfoot t-shirts. Bigfoot hats. Bigfoot memes. Hell, Bigfoot was even used to market jerky. What a joke this was going to be. A seasoned fire crew killed by a marketing scheme. But this was no joke, and these were no cartoon creatures. They were real, and they were deadly.

"Holy shit! My ears are ringing from that. Sorry, I gave you a hard time, Pederson. I guess you were right after all. You did hear something."

Dutch's apology brought a nervous laugh from everyone.

"Your ears might be ringing, but my underwear's stinking."

Wallace was joking, of course. Gallows humor. It might be tacky and crude, but it did loosen everyone's nerves.

"Well, we know one thing's for sure."

"What's that, Cap?"

"We're never gonna doubt Pederson's ears again."

The crew could do nothing but stay put and wait for the inevitable. They all knew they were on borrowed time, and, like everyone who has ever faced their end, their thoughts turned to family, friends, and regrets. Proctor's thoughts covered all of these manifested in one person. A close friend, someone he had just come to understand he loves. And regret. The regret of not letting Nancy know how he felt. He didn't want to leave this earth without telling her. He pulled his pocket notepad out of his shirt and started to write her a note. He didn't know what to write. He stared at that notepad with a blank look. Finally, he just wrote, "I wish I hadn't wasted so much time learning that I love you, Nancy. Forgive me." Then he closed the notepad and returned it to his pocket. Everyone saw it. They all felt this was the end, but seeing a man they respected as a leader and rock succumb to the situation was disheartening.

Captain Robertson needed to get his guys refocused on survival. Once a defeatist attitude set in, surviving the threat would become almost impossible.

"Tell her to her face when we get out of this cave. If you don't, me and the fellas are gonna gang tackle you and take that damn notepad out of your pocket and show it to Mills for you. We ain't dead yet, and I ain't plannin' on goin' out quietly. You got that, Squatch?"

"Ten-four, Cap. You won't need to gang tackle me. First thing I'm gonna do is find her and give her a big ole bear hug."

Proctor needed that little prod from Robertson. They all needed it. There was a renewed sense of purpose, and that purpose was to survive. *All* of them.

11

RELIEF

"Fire base command to fire Team C. Come in, Mills. Fire base command to fire Team C. Are you there, Nance?"

With all the variables of this fire, Nancy had almost forgotten about monitoring the radio. The call startled her back into focus.

"Team C to fire base command. Go ahead."

"Good news, Nance. I've got two choppers heading to load water as we speak. They're heading to the Ponderay from the Bonner's Ferry staging area. Should be on your position in a couple hours or so. When they get on target, pop green smoke, so they know where you are. They'll dump behind your position to try and buy you some more time to break through to the upper service road. Over."

"Ten-four. Sounds great. Have the pilot radio us on this frequency when he clears Dufort Road. I'll pop smoke then. Over."

"Roger, Nance. Will do. Fire base command out."

Nancy turned to Stumpy.

"Well, you heard it yourself. Air strikes are on the way."

Until now, the job seemed an impossible mix of obstacles attempting to foil the crew's every move to suppress the fire and survive the mountain. For the first time since they arrived on this fire, Mills and Stumpy actually felt some measure of relief. Still, there was the unknown of this creature, this Seatco, to deal with. There hadn't been any sign of them for quite a while, and it was nice to have only the sounds of the fire and the efforts of the crews. It was a little disconcerting that they were so quiet.

Mills had that quiet-before-the-storm, feeling in the pit of her stomach. Call it women's intuition or just a heightened sense of awareness, but it would soon be evident that her senses were right. Her thoughts drifted to Ben Proctor and the others holed up in the caverns. She hadn't allowed herself to think about Ben much while conducting the tasks at hand. She couldn't. She seemed to lose focus whenever she thought of Ben. Especially lately. All she could do was hope and pray he and the others were safe.

12

FIRE BASE COMMAND: COEUR D' ALENE

"How soon do you think we can get up there, Pete? If we wait any longer, there won't be any evidence to recover. The damn fire will erase it."

Lieutenant Randy Thomas and his partner, Detective Carl Van Buren, were investigating the missing persons case of Brandon and Steve Rucker. Dispatch had given them the message from Robertson's report of finding the wallet belonging to Brandon Rucker, and some possible remains as well. As far as evidence goes, time is of the essence in any case, but particularly since the fire could eliminate any chance of closing the case with a cause of death.

"Well, lieutenant, you heard the transmission. The fire's raging pretty good, and with the way the wind's been blowin', we're just now starting to get some aerial suppression up there. Gonna be a while. It'll probably be days before you guys could get up there. And that's assuming they get a handle on this fire. There's already been quite a bit of tragedy up there. Something or someone's been harassing the teams, and all we can do is listen. All access to their location is engulfed in fire. They are on their own until we can knock this fire down."

Fire dispatcher Pete Walker was more than a little worried. He had been on duty since the crews were deployed and had been monitoring all the communications on the mountain. He heard all the transmissions regarding the attacks, the injuries, the deaths, and the missing crew members. Something was going on up there. Something besides the fire. With over twenty years experience as a fire dispatcher, he had heard many strange stories about the Hoodoo Mountain area. Everything from strange lights in the sky, space aliens, and even Bigfoot. He had never put much stock in those stories, but now he wasn't so sure. *Something* was up there with the crews, but he sure as hell wasn't going to let the Bonner County Sheriff investigators know what he thought. Not yet. Bigfoot? They'd never let him hear the end of that one.

"All right, Pete. Give us a ring as soon as we can get up there. These boys' families want some answers."

"Will do, Randy. I'll call you as soon as I get the all-clear."

The news of the air drops coming within a couple of hours gave the crews the burst of energy and enthusiasm needed to redouble their efforts. Everyone was moving at an accelerated pace, and they were making good progress up the ridge. Even the fire's pace seemed to slow down as the winds died and shifted direction. For the first time in hours, everything seemed to be improving. They all started to feel they might just get off of this mountain alive. But the mountain wasn't the only thing they were fighting, and they knew it.

Jackson Matoskah and Dave Wilson were running the lead and making good progress. The rest of the crew were making short work of clearing the debris. Boyd Jeffries and Brian Frye were in reserve waiting to relieve Matoskah and Wilson when their saws ran out of fuel. The four of them would continually rotate so they would not become overly fatigued. It was easier on the saws as well. The constant buzz from chainsaws and the sounds of the fire were like a strangely orchestrated concert accentuated with the rhythmic thumping of falling trees. It was quite the dance, and those who had a part in this performance felt privileged and honored to be part of it. After all, they were selflessly saving entire towns, property, and surely people's lives. Everything was going so well, they almost forgot about the other force of nature with them on this mountain. Almost.

It had been over ninety minutes since the last contact with fire base command, and Mills was getting anxious for contact from the pilot to let her know when the first air drop would come. Even though the fire had slowed, it hadn't stopped its steady progression towards the ridge top. It had already overtaken the rocky outcrop where Captain Robertson's group had been just a couple of hours earlier, and it wouldn't be long before it caught up with this crew as well. If they could start water drops within the next hour or two, it could buy them enough time to clear the path all the way to the fire service road above them. Then they could go back on offense and turn the fire back on itself. The water drops were key. They usually were.

"Air One to Hoodoo fire crew. Air One to Hoodoo fire crew. Copy?"

Lieutenant Commander Martin "Al" Peak, a veteran of numerous helicopter missions over northern Iraq, was at the controls of the helicopter carrying the first of what would be a constant barrage of water drops by him and his partner, Lieutenant Walter Winslow, also a veteran of many combat missions. They were not strangers to flying in dangerous conditions. They may not have been under fire from enemy forces, but large fires like this one could create changing wind patterns and sudden heat vortexes. Not to mention the restricted visibility from the heavy smoke.

"I copy, Air One. Mills here. You sure are a welcome voice. Where you at? Over."

"We're approaching the Ponderay and will be scooping water in about twenty minutes. Hopefully we'll be over your twenty in half an hour or so. We'll be there before sunrise. Can you throw a couple strobes out to mark your position? Over."

"Ten-four, Air One. Roger, two strobes. Over."

"Hey, Stumpy, are you ready to take a shower?"

During water drops, there always seemed to be some overspray, and if it happened to drop on the crews, it offered a short respite from the heat and the grit and grime of the fire lines.

"Hey, Pitts, grab two strobes from the kit and put them out in that cleared-out area to the west of our trucks."

"On it, Nance."

Brian Pitts was what many would call an eager beaver. As one of the newbies on Nancy's team, he was always on the "go-for" list. It was a right of passage for all rookie members. Before anyone could be trusted with bigger responsibilities, they had to prove themselves willing and able to handle all manner of lesser tasks — fetching water for the crews, gathering tools, and anything else the more seasoned crew members didn't want to do. There was always some friendly teasing and trash talk from the crew. It was the way it had always been and would always be. It was about team building and camaraderie, which eventually built trust and a sense of brotherhood — one might even say family. The rookies were more than happy to play this role, and Pitts was especially enthusiastic.

Pitts was so eager to do this task with speed, he just about fell over his own feet as he ran into the dark to place the strobes.

"Rookies." Boyd Jeffries shook his head and quietly laughed at Pitts' clumsy start.

"Don't get lost out there in the dark, rook. I ain't coming out there to get you if you do."

Everyone at the command trucks chuckled uneasily. Although it had been quiet for some time, they couldn't shake the feeling they were being watched. And Pitts was running into the darkness alone. Everyone strained their eyes to try and see him as he placed the strobes. There wasn't much they could do if something attacked him out there. Shotguns were a great weapon, but they were not surgical weapons. If they were to shoot at an attacker, they might be shooting Pitts, too.

It was only one or two minutes, but to all the crew straining to see Pitts activate the strobes, it seemed much longer. The first strobe pierced the dark and started its rhythmic flashing. The smoke from the fires created an eerie halo effect around the light. Then, the second strobe started flashing a short distance from the first. The two lights seemed to be synchronized and keeping a cadence with a silent beat. They flashed, not at the same time, but more like in a synco-pated, staccato rhythm. Even though the strobes were extremely bright, the smoke toned down the area they illuminated, and no one could see Pitts as he ran back towards the command area.

From his vantage point just above the trespassers below, the alpha could see everything the intruders were doing. He had no way of knowing those very intruders were actually there to help save the lands he and his kind had reigned over for millennia. All the alpha knew was these trespassers were destroying their world. He didn't know that they were in no way connected to the ones who started the fire. From what he had witnessed, they were of the same tribe, and all this tribe knew how to do was destroy nature and threaten the very existence of his tribe with this destruction. It was his duty to protect the tribe and the tribal lands from all who would not respect it. Too many times, he and those before him had seen this tribe abuse the lands and the lives of those who lived there. He had seen them kill just to kill. He had seen them disrespect life by taking only the heads of some of the ones they killed, leaving the rest to spoil. The tribe always tried to salvage the remains for their own use, but it was not always the case. Yes, the scavengers of the lands would find it, and what was left would feed them. But for one tribe to waste such a life was unconscionable. His tribe did not differentiate one human from another. As far as the tribe was concerned, all humans belonged to the same tribe, and that tribe had no respect for life or the natural ways of things.

That was not to say that he had not seen some act with respect. There were those who didn't leave things in the woods, those who took out what they brought in, those who didn't put their marks on rocks and trees and who respected the life of the prey they harvested. But that tribe seemed to be getting less and less respectful of the land and the creatures that inhabited it.

As for the trespassers below, their time was running out. Tribal justice would soon erase them from their lands. Soon, the other males would signal they were in position, and the alpha would move in. The tribe took no joy in killing for killing's sake, if joy was an emotion they felt. Killing, for them, was a way to feed the tribe, was necessary for survival, and only done when needed. The only other time killing was acceptable was in defense of their lands and their way of life. Such was the situation they faced on this day.

It wouldn't be long. Not long at all.

13

MONIKER

"I can see the finish line, Nance." Welch, aka Toothless, was at the front of the clearing efforts. He could see the old fire service road only fifty or so yards away. The trees were thinning, and he could make out the unmistakable space in the forest the road created.

"Good job, Toothless. Let me know when we can move the trucks up."

"Will do, Nance. Hopefully before sunrise."

"Sounds good. You guys will be glad to hear I just got off the horn with the choppers bringing our water drop. Should be here in less than an hour. Hope you're ready for a shower."

The sight of the fire service road and the news of the water drop coming soon energized the crew, and what was an exhausted and deflated group of fire fighters became a laser-focused, highly motivated crew.

"All right, ladies. Last one to the top buys the first round of beers." Toothless was in no way going to be the last one up. He enjoyed his cold brews and savored them even more when someone else paid.

"What'd I miss, guys." Jackson Matoskah had just made it back to the front lines after painting the equipment.

"We're almost to the breakout point. The fire service road is just ahead." Matoskah could see the excitement on Spud's face as well as on everyone else.

Matoskah still needed to paint the helmets of these guys before they went any further. It had been quiet on the creature front for some time, and he knew this would not sit well with the crew.

"Well, before we move up, I need to mark your hard hats."

Toothless was first to speak up.

"What kind of artwork are you putting on the hard hats? What's the deal, Jack?"

Matoskah knew he was going to get ragged on, but he didn't have a choice and didn't have much time.

"It's a tribal protection totem. Hopefully, it will help protect us from whatever is on this mountain. It's the totem of its tribe, I think. Anyway, just humor me on this one."

"You can paint up all the hats you want, but you ain't touchin' my damn hard hat. To hell with all that Native shit." Toothless was adamant. He didn't put much stock in good luck charms, folklore, or Old World mumbo-jumbo.

"C'mon, Toothless. Mills said to do it."

"You got Nance buying this crap? Geez, Jack. I know you're Native and all, but this is just plain idiotic."

"I get it, Toothless. But what if— just what if it works?"

Toothless stood there, mulling it over. "It's bullshit, and I ain't wearin' no damn stupid painting on my hat." With that, Toothless picked up his saw and moved up to the next line of trees to be cut.

The others weren't so firm in their thoughts. Larry Carter was first to hand Matoskah his hard hat, and the rest fell in line. Matoskah got right to work. Thank goodness the marking was so simple and easy to duplicate. It didn't take long to get everyone's done, and, one by one as their hard hats were adorned, they moved up the line and got back to work.

With his brief assignment as crew artist finished, Matoskah grabbed his saw and also rejoined the front line. At first, the crew was silent except for the buzzing of the chainsaws. But it didn't take long before the crew was talking about the logo. They even came up with nicknames for their crew and its new moniker.

"Hey, how about Squatch Fighters?" Craig Stephens' entry into the hat was greeted with moans and groans.

"I got it," Gordon "Gordo" Nelson chimed in. "How 'bout Fire Squatchers?" Gordo's entry was met with similar results.

"Geez, Gordo, that sounds like we're all sufferin' from a case of jalapeño fire craps." Stumpy always had a way of looking at the off side of everything. It kind of went with the job, a skewed sense of humor.

Everyone was still laughing and joking about Stumpy's comment when a man of few words, Dave Wilson, put his idea out there.

"Fire Devils."

Everyone was taken aback by Wilson's input. He had a way of getting to the point without using any unnecessary words.

Almost on cue, the crew offered their approval for Wilson's suggestion.

The irony of the name was not lost on Jackson Matoskah. Fire Devils. They were fighting a fire on a mountain named Hoodoo, meaning mountain devil or demon in some Native American tribes, while also fighting an unseen devil or beast. The name seemed appropriate.

Stumpy struck a haughty pose and, with his hard hat placed over his heart, proclaimed, "I now present to the world, the Fire Devils of the Idaho Panhandle Fire Management crew. May their days be many."

The crew seemed happy with their new name. All except Toothless. He was indignant.

"You guys have lost your ever-lovin' minds." Toothless was the only dissenting voice and the only one without the totem of the Seatco on his hard hat. His lack of belief in what Jackson Matoskah had to say would prove to be a terrible mistake. Except for the steady roar from the ever-closing flames of the fire raging below them, and the rhythmic buzz from the crew's chainsaws, all was eerily quiet.

14

THE SIGNAL

The tactics were simple: get the trespassers to focus away from where the attack would start, then move in closer. Create another diversion from another direction so others could move in closer, then do it again and again until they were close enough to attack from all sides. Swift, efficient, and deadly. The first signal would come from somewhere just below the trespassers. This would come from one of the beta males and would signal the alpha that all tribe members were in position. This signal would also allow the alpha to move in from above, where he would signal, and then others would move in from one of the flanks, and then they would signal. At this point, others would move in from the other flank. It wouldn't take long to get close enough to strike.

The alpha sat still, waiting for the first signal. It would be a long howl. Loud and deeply pitched, it would include something devastating: infrasound.

This is a tone that the human ear cannot hear. Infrasound sound waves are emitted with the guttural growls and roars from many apex predators such as tigers, lions, and other large cats, as well as from bears and the larger members of the ape family. Infrasound serves to briefly stun the intended prey or instill a deep sense of fear to drive away rival predators or warn off challenges for position from junior members of a group. The tone affects the human body in various ways. It can create severe headaches, nausea, and an overwhelming physical sense of dread. But the most common reaction is to be stunned, unable to move. Although these effects are usually short-lived, it allows tribe members to get in close and attack before there can be a reaction from the intended target. This is how they hunt. Infrasound stuns their prey just long enough so that they can move in quickly for a swift kill and avoid the defenses of their prey — antlers, in the case of deer and other ungulates. Imagine a 200-pound animal using twenty-four-inch or longer bone spears. Bears, lions, and other predators have teeth and claws that can injure or kill. Infrasound helps minimize these defenses. Most of the time.

Many of the male tribe members carried scars on their bodies from hunting and defending their group. Even the alpha had many battle scars. Scars showed the other members of the tribe how capable of providing and protection one was. And, maybe more importantly, they showed other tribes they might encounter that they were not to be challenged.

There are very few conflicts between rival tribes. Their very structure of being minimal in group size and the wide-spread territory they inhabit make for a balance of power. Yes, infrasound is a vital tool for the tribe. Especially when their target has thunder sticks, which can kill or maim from a distance. This is why the weapon of choice for the tribe has been large rocks that can be thrown from the shadows or other places of cover.

He could see the trespassers clearly now. They were almost to the ridge top. The others should have been close to being in position. The alpha sat and patiently waited, motionless, unblinking. The only movement was created by the wind moving the hair that covered his body.

Then, from somewhere below the trespassers came the first howl. The depth and tenor of resonated throughout the forest. It penetrated the bodies of the trespassers and rocked their souls. The alpha did not hesitate. In seconds ,he had moved unseen over fifty yards closer. Before the signal howl had even finished, he was in position. His howl would be even more powerful and disruptive.

15

STUNNED

The lead crew was still bantering back and forth over their new logo when the signal howl emanated from far below the command truck. Even at that distance, the effects of the infrasound were felt. It vibrated deep within their bodies and, to a man, caused them to freeze. It confused them, even if only for a few seconds; the feeling of extreme dread and fear it created was palpable.

"What the fuck?" Toothless expressed what they were all thinking. They had all but forgotten about the creature, hoping it was done.

"I thought we were rid of all this bullshit. So much for your fuckin' protection mark, Jack. I told you guys it was total crap." Toothless was uncharacteristically unhinged. It was understandable but not good. Everyone had seen him in many dangerous situations in the past. He was always cool under pressure. That's what infrasound could do to a person. It could disorient and confuse the victim, which could lead to unnatural reactions. Seeing Toothless lose his cool set everyone into a deeper panic.

Stumpy knew if the crew panicked, their chances of survival would greatly diminish. He had to get them to focus.

"Settle down, Toothless. Everybody, settle down. We have a shotgun, and we have chainsaws. Anything comes in here, it's gonna get a whirlwind of problems. Let's just pull in and make a circle. No blind spots."

Stumpy's little pep talk calmed most of the crew, but Toothless was rattled. The sudden fear and surprise caused by the infrasound in the howl had done its job. He was confused, and confusion often leads to poor decisions and panic. Panic is a predator's best ally. Panic fogs reasonable thought and blocks the ability to control the emotions. Toothless was almost in panic mode; he couldn't get a grip on his fear, and his thoughts came rushing out of his mouth without regard for the others' own struggles to keep their heads. This could cause the whole crew to panic.

"Form a fuckin' circle? What good will that do? Haven't you been pay in' attention? This damn thing isn't alone. There's more than one out there. Shit! Shit! What the fuck?"

Stumpy ran up to Toothless and back-handed him as hard as he could, a risky move considering Toothless' size and penchant for fighting. But it was all he knew to do.

"Get a damn grip, Toothless! We've got to stick together."

It took a couple seconds for Toothless to come back from the edge, but Stumpy's slap seemed to jar the effects from the infrasound from him. He just blinked, shook the fog from his head, walked a few feet away from the crew, lit a cigarette, and stared into the darkness beyond the glow of the fires below.

As bad as the reaction from the infrasound by Toothless was, the crew members at the command truck had been even closer to the howl. They got a much stronger dose. Some of the crew suddenly felt a slight nausea, the type of nervous stomach similar to the feeling some people get when they hit the first big drop on a roller-coaster. Nancy Mills received an instant, piercing pain right between the eyes that had her briefly doubled over. She almost dropped her shotgun but quickly regained her focus and composure.

"Get behind the trucks! I want eyes on all sides. Damn, that was awful close. Anyone see Pitts?"

As if on cue, Pitts stumbled back into the protective area between the two trucks. He quickly regained his feet and staggered to a position behind one of the trucks, facing the direction of the howl. With most of the crew up ahead clearing a path, there was only six people at command: Brian Pitts, Tim Yancey, Lloyd Davidson, Boyd Jeffries, Steve Parsons, and Mills. But they did have two shotguns, so Mills had Yancey positioned facing downhill with one while she held the other one. Staying in the center of the two trucks, she could turn to face any threat in any direction.

"Jesus Christ! It felt like that thing was right behind me." Pitts was wide-eyed and hyperventilating, not so much from the running, but from the adrenaline rush and the pounding of his heart from the infrasound. Everyone at the command area had experienced some effect from it. The most prevalent effects were a sense of dread and an overwhelming fear.

"It's coming, guys. Let's hope Jack's idea works, 'cause we're gonna find out pretty damn quick."

They had positioned their two trucks in a loose V formation with the sides facing up and downhill. Matoskah had made the totems large in hopes they could be seen from a long way off. If this idea was going to work, making the totem easy to see from a distance just might save them.

Mills hoped the helicopters with water drops would be there soon. Having eyes in the sky might give them an edge. Now, how would they inform the pilots what was happening?

The alpha had closed in to just over a hundred yards of the trespassers. When he let loose his howl, the two flanking tribe members would close in, and the trespasser's time in their lands would be soon be done. Their bodies would be left to the fire, and then the scavengers would clean up.

This has been the way for as long as the tribe has been on the mountain. It is how it has always been for all the tribes throughout the world. This is why they have been able to stay mostly hidden from the rest of the world. Nothing is left. The birds signal all others by their circling and noisy chatter while they pick at the remains. Then the larger meat eaters come in; coyotes, wolves, bears, and lions each have a turn. They drag bits and prices away in all directions, effectively erasing all evidence of the carnage. Even small rodents gnaw on the bones to get their supply of calcium. Then the bugs come by the thousands and quickly reduce what's left to the bare minimum. Then the birds return, eating the bugs and carrying away anything left. And so, the cycle of life plays out. Everything has its purpose.

The howl from the alpha was deep. Very deep. It seemed to shake the rocks and trees right down to the ground. This howl was more like a roar. The crew members felt it resonate up from the depths of the mountain and pierce their bodies like so many bees buzzing through their souls. They were all briefly immobilized, not only by fear, but also from the other, more stubborn effects of the infrasound on their bodies. The crew also felt unable to focus their thoughts and had piercing headaches.

The two flankers moved swiftly and quietly to their final position. They gathered large stones to strike the trespassers with from a distance. When the alpha signaled for attack to begin, it would be he who would strike the first blow. The betas would only move in closer after their enemy was disorganized and reeling from the sudden attack. It was the alpha's responsibility to protect the tribe. They had already lost one member, and with the tribe being limited in number, they could not stand to lose too many young males. So, the alpha would keep the attack on the trespassers limited to striking from a safe distance and stay to the shadows to conceal their positions. They would throw large rocks from these protected positions to inflict the initial injuries. Even though it was not the most effective way to ensure a kill, breaking the neck was the usual way. It was quick and, if the target did survive, they would be rendered helpless and unable to injure the tribe members.

It was the alpha's turn to move.

Again, the beta below the crew howled, but this time he was joined by the two flanking males. This would completely disorient the trespassers and allow the alpha to move to within striking distance in silence.

"Holy shit! It sounds like there's *twenty* of those things out there." Pitts had just settled in behind the downhill truck.

"You tellin' me I was out there with those *things*? How come I didn't see nothin'? I know it's dark and smokey, but that's close as hell."

"You're right, Pitts. You'd think we could see *something* if they were that close. Where the hell *are* they? If I could just get one in my sights, I might be able to get a shot at it." Yancey was eager to get a shot off at whatever was coming for them. His and the others' imaginations were running rampant, trying to picture what these creatures were and what they looked like. The question of why they were being attacked wasn't part of the conversation.

Except by Matoskah. Even though he was not currently active in the Kalispel tribal traditions, he had been raised in the tribe and been told the stories that have been passed down from generation to generation. These included the tales of the Seatco and, although few, tales of interactions with the Kalispel who ventured into the Seatco's lands. It had been quite a while since he had heard the stories, and he might not have all the answers, but he hoped he had at least one answer, the sign of the Seatco. If he had remembered these stories correctly, it could be their only chance to survive. Matoskah felt the attacks were because of perceived destruction of the Seatco's land. It all seemed to add up. After all, the fire was started by two people lighting off fireworks within what the Seatco claimed as their land. And it appeared those two individuals may have already been punished. Now the fire crews had come into their lands and started cutting trees and starting back-burns. In Matoskah's mind, these actions might have looked as though the fire crews were also damaging their lands. There would be no way they could understand that the fire crews were there to help *stop* the destruction. There wasn't any time for him to ponder the reasons or possible solutions to their situation; the howls and calls from the tribe would keep Jack and the others just trying to find a way to survive.

16

FIRST BLOW

Toothless was still smoking his cigarette and was out from the crew and their circle. He had turned and started back to the others when he was hit by a softball-size rock. It came from out of nowhere, striking him right on the back of his hard hat, knocking Toothless off his feet. He rolled, unconscious, towards the others. The timing of his movement was the only reason he wasn't killed instantly. Instead of being struck on the left side of his skull and having his head crushed at the temple, his turning shifted the striking point to the back of his head. Toothless had tilted his hard hat back on his head while he was smoking, so the force of the rock was absorbed by his hard hat. Even so, it knocked him out and gave him a concussion. And he broke his collarbone when he fell, but he was alive. Before anyone could move to get him, two more large stones came flying in. One hit Austin Matthews in the throat, crushing his windpipe. This would prove fatal. The other stone just missed Stumpy's head as he turned to help Matthews. If he hadn't moved, he would also have been struck and probably killed or seriously injured.

Stumpy turned, blindly aimed his shotgun in the direction of the projectiles, and let loose two blasts into the dark.

"Jesus! Jesus! Someone help me get Toothless behind cover." Brian Frye and Larry Carter sprung into action to drag Toothless behind a large red fir tree. Craig Stephens had made it to Matthews just as he choked out his last, labored breath. And Matthews was gone. Stephens briefly hesitated before dropping and rolling behind a nearby boulder, losing his hard hat.

"Damnit!" He knew his hard hat was the best protection he had from the stone missiles flying in.

Crash! Another stone shattered against the boulder he was hiding behind.

"Holy shit! That rock just disintegrated." He had never seen rocks the size of these fragment like that. These were not sandstone or highly fractured stones. They were granite.

Soon after the rock shattered, there came another howl. This one sounded within just a few feet of the terrified fire crew. It was the signal from the alpha for the others to start their air assault.

The crew at the command trucks knew the forward crew was under attack. They heard the yelling and the two shotgun blasts. There was nothing they could do to help them. When the howl erupted from the forward team's location, they knew all hell was getting ready to break loose. They were right.

Bam! Bam! Bam! The large stones seemed to be coming from all directions. Four stones struck the two command trucks almost at the same time. These stones were basketball- and football-size, and the impact on the trucks was impressive. Steve Parsons had taken cover behind the driver's side, front quarter panel. His right hand was resting on the fender when — *bam!* One of the rocks landed squarely on the fender, smashing two fingers on SP's right hand. Normally, it would have been a safe spot, as the wheel and the engine provided additional protection. It was just a one-in-a-million chance that SP would get injured by a well-thrown rock. The other three stones left marks on the trucks as well. But the only injury was to SP's fingers.

Mills was trying to maintain control of the crew and keep them safe, if possible.

"Keep your heads down! We don't know where these things are, and I don't want to give them any easy targets."

Her warning would come too late for Lloyd Davidson. Davidson wasn't in the best cover. He was exposed at the rear of the uphill truck and in full view of one of the betas on the flank. He never saw the stone that crushed his skull. It hit with such force that his head was almost flattened. Death was instant.

Paul Meyer was closest to Davidson when he was hit. Blood spattered Meyer from Davidson's head exploding, and he lost control. "Oh my god! Son of a bitch. He's *dead*. He's dead! I got his brains all over me. Get it off me! Get it the hell off me!" Meyer tried to wipe the remnants of Davidson off himself, all the while shaking and rambling incoherently.

"Meyer! Get ahold of yourself! Get over to Yancey's position and get the hell behind better cover," Mills directed from her cover position, where the two trucks met and formed a V. It was good cover from three sides, but the back ends of the trucks were spread open, leaving the crew exposed to attack from the south.

The alpha was moving from side to side and launching stones from slightly different angles to confuse the trespassers and not let them know exactly where he was. His attack was swift and effective. The two blasts from the thunder sticks came nowhere near where the alpha was. He had moved to a more-or-less flanking position after starting his attack from the front. He was just about to restart his attack, when he saw it: the marking on the side of one of the hard hats. The alpha froze mid-motion, his raised arm trembling as his mind struggled to process what his eyes were seeing.

The markings were *his* tribal symbol. Only those who knew of the tribe would know about the marking. Only those who understood the tribe's ways would mark themselves with the mark of the tribe. He hadn't seen this in his lifetime. He only knew of this through the tribal lore passed down from the ancient ones.

Even though they didn't have a complex language, like humans, they *did* have a rudimentary language. This language was confined to basic tones and vocalizations and augmented with wood knocks and a basic sign language. The sign language was not filled with letters or words. It was more pictorial in nature. Information was relayed from tribe member to tribe member in this way. And this is how the ancient tribe members communicated with others that were not of their species. In their distant past, the tribe would occasionally have contact with human tribes. These tribes had a mutual, basic understanding and belief system that revolved around respect — respect for the lands and the creatures living within them. This understanding slowly faded, the human tribes disappeared, and a different human tribe emerged. This tribe knew nothing of the old ways and knew nothing about respect.

The alpha searched the others and saw the tribal mark on all of them. He would stop the attack, for now. He would signal the betas to stop their attack too. The signal was simple, basic. Three loud, short, whoops.

Even though this signal was a sign of a ceasefire of sorts, the fire crew didn't feel any better when they heard the sounds.

The betas answered with three whoops to signal that they understood and would stop their attacks. In a matter of seconds, all aggression from the tribe stopped, and silence enveloped the mountain — an eerie, uneasy, silence that put the crews even more on edge.

"Why'd they stop?" Carter was asking what everyone was wondering. Why stop the attack when the attackers had the upper hand? It didn't make sense.

"Everyone stay where you are. Keep Toothless covered and make sure nothing else's busted on him." Stumpy knew he had to keep his crew focused, so their minds were busy. He reloaded more shells to make sure the shotgun was fully loaded, ready for the next attack.

At the command trucks, Nancy Mills assessed her crew's situation. They had lost a man and had another man injured. It wasn't looking too good. She knew there was more than one creature attacking their position, and with only five crew left, they probably wouldn't survive long when the next attack came. But they were sure going to put up a fight.

"Hey, SP, you okay?"

It was kind of a joke among the crew. SP was always damaging his fingers, one way or another. Cuts, splinters, breaks, dislocations — he always seemed to have his fingers bandaged or taped up.

"Yeah, looks like I got a couple of broken fingers. Figures."

Paul Meyer headed over to check on Spud's fingers.

"Yep. You busted them good. I'll splint them up for ya'. Gonna hurt." Meyer grabbed the first aid kit out of the truck and splinted and taped SP's fingers as straight as he could. Then he taped the two fingers together to keep them from moving too much and doing more damage.

"Damn, that hurt. Easy on the ole fingers, Meyer. Jesus *Christ!*"

"Quit your bitchin', SP. Ain't like you never screwed your fingers up. Should be used to your fingers hurtin' by now."

"Hey, Yancey, get up in the truck and work that spotlight. See if you can see anything out there. But keep your head on a swivel."

The trucks were all equipped with roof-mounted spotlights that swiveled 360 degrees. These lights had three-million-candle-power beams and could light up a huge area. They could even cut through pretty thick smoke.

Yancey made his way to the truck facing downhill and switched on the spotlight. He scanned as much of the area as the light would reach. Nothing.

"What the hell? These things were pretty damn close, and I don't see *anything* out there, Nance. Where'd they go?"

"Who knows? Keep searching. Might catch a glimpse of what we're up against."

The alpha was thinking on what to do next. Nothing like this had ever come about in his lifetime. With the exception of the rare, accidental contact or tribal intervention with trespassers, there had never been any contact with the human tribes. It had happened in the tribe's historical past, but those encounters were generations ago. He wasn't sure how to proceed.

17

THE VISION

Jimmy Two Horns and the other Kalispel elders were keeping their vigil at the access road that led up into the Hoodoo mountains. They felt the change in the winds coming long before they actually reached the mountain. Now they sensed — some would say, they actually saw — the events unfolding high up the mountain. Two Horns' gaze suddenly became fixed in a faraway stare, as if he was watching events at a great distance. He stopped his chant and stood, motionless, for several minutes. The others stopped as well, knowing Two Horns was in a trance, or waking dream state, often called a vision quest. Once obtained, the state needed total focus to maintain.

Two Horns stood there as if paralyzed for several minutes. His silence was broken by Two Horns himself. He started repeating the word *see* over and over. As he did this, the others walked around him in a circle holding burning sage. The smoke from the sage engulfed him, and still he chanted, "See." This went on for half an hour, until Two Horns fell to the ground unconscious. Just before he collapsed, the sage smoke suddenly cleared, as if carrying his single-word message up the mountain.

This is the story as told by the Kalispel. It is not disputed.

18

THE OLIVE BRANCH

About the time of Jimmy Two Horn's trance, Jackson Matoskah was having a strange event of his own. In the dead silence surrounding him and the others, he thought he heard a voice on the wind. A whisper. He figured it was just his nerves playing tricks on his mind. He didn't have time to ponder it long. His thoughts were interrupted by an object that appeared out of the darkness. At first, he thought another attack was starting. But the object wasn't a well-aimed rock coming in with tremendous force. It was a branch. Or, rather, a piece of a branch. It didn't come in like an attack, but as if gently lobbed in. It landed just a few feet from where Toothless was being tended to, scaring Stumpy and Larry Carter half to death. This, in itself, was strange. But what happened next was unnerving. From somewhere past where they could see but very close, too close, came a short, high-pitched whoop. Just one, and nothing else. Everyone froze, not knowing what to make of it. Matoskah was the first to move, as if by an unseen force. He felt he had to see what this stick was all about.

"Jack! What the hell are you doing? That thing's pretty damn close. Get the hell back under cover." Stumpy's words didn't stop Matoskah from continuing towards the stick.

"It's okay, Stumpy. I don't think this is a bad thing."

"Be careful, Jack. Eyes open. I got you covered."

Matoskah crept slowly towards the stick. He felt his nervous sweat running down the back of his neck. His heart was pounding so hard, he could hear it. At first, he was reluctant to turn on his headlamp, but as he got to the stick, he decided to use his light to get a close look at it. When he picked it up, he saw something scratched into the wood. This wasn't some tiny little stick. It was about four inches around and eighteen inches long. As he rolled the stick in his hands, he saw what was scratched into the wood. It was the same thing he had seen scratched into the old tree. The same thing he had drawn on everyone's hard hats and the trucks. The mark of the Seatco. A chill ran through his body. It wasn't fear so much as the excitement one gets from the sudden rush of adrenaline. Fight or flight. This was not going to be a fight; nor would they be able to run. Matoskah turned to Stumpy with a look of shock. He slowly raised the stick and shone his light on the marking.

"It's the same as what's on our hard hats, Stumpy. It's the mark of the Seatco. The watcher. The mountain demon. It must've seen the mark on the hard hats. I think it wants to... I don't know... communicate somehow. Why else would it do this?"

"You're nuts, Jack. This thing's been trying to wipe us off this damn mountain, and all of a sudden it wants to play nicey-nice? I don't think so. I think it's just trying to make it easy on itself and making us come out into the open."

"Stumpy, I know this is gonna sound crazy, but my grandfather told me stories of the tribe of the woods, the Seatco, and how they were kind of protectors of the woods. He said they used to have occasional contact with this tribe. It wasn't often, but they knew to respect the Seatco's ways. They would put this totem on their quivers or other clothing to honor them. They would leave offerings to the tribe if they needed to enter their lands. These ways have been forgotten by most, including me. But after the attacks began, and we came across this totem scratched on trees and into boulders, I remembered my grandfather's stories. That's why I painted our hard hats. I think it's seen the totem, and that's why the attack stopped, and I think this stick is a sign. A sign it wants to meet. Radio Mills. See what's going on with them. I bet it's quiet down there, too."

Stumpy had bewilderment on his face. First, he couldn't believe what he was hearing, and, second, he was actually thinking Matoskah could be right.

"Okay, Jack. Let's check in with Nance, and we'll go from there. Stumpy to Mills. Nance, you there?"

"We're here, Sam. We've lost Davidson, and Spud's hurt, but we're hangin' on. Weird, though. Everything just stopped, and it's real quiet. I don't like it."

"Ten-four, Nance. Same here. Matthews is down, and Toothless is busted up a bit, but it's quiet. Except for one thing..."

Stumpy told Mills about the stick and the marking on it, and he told her Matoskah's idea on the subject.

"Jack wants to see if this *Seatco* wants to make contact. What do you want to do? He's your guy."

"Well, Stumpy, if he's right, it could be our ticket off this mountain. If he's wrong, well, we're all probably dead anyway. I say, let him try. But keep a close watch on him. Cover him."

"Roger. Will keep you posted."

"Well, Jack, you're on."

All of a sudden, Matoskah felt as though the lives of the entire fire crew were in his hands. He wasn't even sure what he was going to do or how to "talk" to this thing. All he had to go on were the stories his grandfather had told him, and they were sketchy at best. He'd been very young when he heard those stories. Memories have a habit of changing over time, especially since the last time he had heard them, he was less than ten years old. One thing was certain — they had gotten him this far. Now, could he finish?

Matoskah picked up the stick, raised it over his head, and walked into the darkness towards where the stick had come from. His knees were like jelly.

The alpha watched the stick land. He had seen the trespasser pick it up and knew the trespasser understood. He could see them talking, and he waited. The alpha would not go to the trespassers. These were *their* lands. It was up to the trespassers to come to him. Then he saw the one who picked up the stick start to come his way. He would sit still and wait for him to get close, very close, before making himself known. The alpha needed to be sure the trespassers wouldn't attack *him*. The trespasser kept coming.

Matoskah faded into the night. The only part of him visible was the outline of his head created by the headlamp. The further he went, the more alone he felt. It didn't matter how much firepower was behind him. If this creature wanted to kill him, nothing could stop it. As he inched deeper into the night, an odor overpowered his senses. He knew the stories of the terrible smell this creature gave off. And now, he remembered it. It was the same one he had smelled on his deer hunt on this very mountain so many years ago. It was a smell he couldn't forget, and here it was again. He knew he was close.

The alpha watched him move closer. Soon, he would reveal himself. As the trespasser approached, the alpha sensed they had been this close before. There was a familiar scent from the trespasser, and he looked familiar. The tribe didn't remember past events as humans did. They remembered smells, sounds, and even faces. But they only remembered in the sense of whether it was good or bad. This memory seemed good. The trespasser was almost in position. He would be able to reveal himself without the other trespassers seeing him.

Matoskah sensed he was about to face what many call Bigfoot, in a context unknown in modern times. He took one more cautious step, when it rose up on its two legs, as if materializing from the ground itself. It towered over Matoskah, and he could feel its breath upon him. It was huge and covered in mottled, white hair. Its face was not humanlike, nor was it apelike. The look was certainly wild, but there was a sense it had an understanding, an intelligence. This being in front of him must have been nine feet tall or more and had to weigh a thousand pounds.

As wild a sight as it was, there was something about the eyes. Matoskah couldn't quite put his finger on it, but it was almost as if it knew him. Recognition? Is that possible? Was this the very creature Matoskah had almost seen on that hunt? There wouldn't be time to wonder. The creature glared at him and bared his teeth, which were long and sharp, and the drool flowed as if it was looking forward to its next meal.

Then it gave a sharp, low-pitched huff. The creature pointed towards the fire and gave out the same angry huff. Then it pointed at Matoskah and started snapping branches and leaving them on the ground. Another huff. At this point, it seemed to wait for Matoskah to respond.

Matoskah was stunned and suddenly felt unprepared. He had no idea what to do next. The creature in front of him seemed to get angry. It snapped more branches and laid them on the ground. Another huff came, only louder. Matoskah felt his thoughts leave him. He started to feel dizzy as the adrenaline and blood flooded his body. He felt about to pass out. The creature leaned in towards him, as if saying, "Well? What have you got to say?"

Matoskah knew he needed to do something, but what? Then, he thought he heard the voice he had heard earlier. What was it saying?

"See... See..."

He heard the words whispered directly into his ear. See *what*? He looked at the sticks on the ground. Then, it hit him. Those sticks were *trees*! It was saying they were cutting down the trees. It didn't understand they were trying to save the forest. It thought they were *destroying* the forest. Now Matoskah had to find a way to make it see what they were really doing. He thought for a few seconds. Then he remembered his grandfather saying they understood visually — a sign language of sorts.

Matoskah picked up the sticks and stuck a bunch in the ground. Then he pointed to the fire and made a hand gesture, wiggling his fingers like flames, and pointed to the sticks in the ground. Now, with his wiggling fingers, he started knocking down the sticks. Then, he reset the sticks in the ground, pointed to himself and towards the others, and laid the sticks closest to the fire down, creating a firebreak by separating the sticks. He then did his wiggling-finger flames but stopped when he got to the sticks still standing.

The alpha stared at what Matoskah had done for a bit. Then he looked at Matoskah, as if staring into his soul. All time seemed to stop. Matoskah didn't even hear the roar of the fire anymore. Everything was hanging on this interaction between man and beast. Was it even possible for them to understand each other? Matoskah had ringing in his ears from the stress and weight of this moment. He felt this massive beast in front of him would strike out at him at any moment; there would be know way to stop it.

All of a sudden, the alpha leaned in even closer and inhaled deeply through his nose. He could smell the fear on this trespasser thick on his body. That was to be expected. But the alpha was also studying this trespasser's body language. He saw that this trespasser, even though there was tremendous fear, had still come to the alpha. He came with nothing in his hands but the stick the alpha had thrown. The alpha leaned back and stood straight up with a short, breathy, grunt. He understood.

19

TREATY

Jackson Matoskah had been gone for about thirty minutes, and the crew feared he'd been killed. But if so, why hadn't the attack restarted? Why was the mountain so quiet? Whatever was going on, the fire wasn't going to wait. They wouldn't be able to stay still much longer.

Stumpy's radio crackled to life.

"Stumpy, this is Jack. We're coming in, so don't shoot. It's all good."

"Ten-four, Jack. What do you mean, 'We're coming in'?"

"You'll see. It's okay, Stumpy."

The crew all turned to Stumpy with the same look of concern. They all got up and headed for Stumpy's position. Safety in numbers. Even Toothless was coming around.

Craig Stephens was the first to see him.

"I see Jack's headlamp. Here he comes. What the...? Holy shit!"

Right behind Matoskah was the alpha. The immense size of the alpha made Jackson appear small, like a child walking with a parent.

The looks on the crew's faces went from concerned to disbelief, then fear. But Stumpy kept the shotgun pointed down. He had to believe Matoskah knew what he was doing.

"You okay, Jack?" he asked but never stopped looking at the creature behind him.

"I'm good, Stumpy. I think. Best I can figure, this is what my people called Seatco. They've been here since the beginning. This mountain is where they live, and they don't put up with anyone destroying it. At least, that's what the stories say. As far as I can figure, it thought we were destroying their lands by cutting trees and doing our back-burns. Had to look bad."

"So... you can talk with it?"

"Not really. It's more of visual communications with grunts and stuff. Not really sure exactly how it works, but we seemed to figure it out. I'm not sure why it followed me back here. It just started walking when I did, so here we are." Matoskah's voice was a little shaky. Even, now, he wasn't completely sure they got it all right.

The alpha just stood there, scanning the faces of the others. Then, he suddenly shifted his gaze to the sky. His body language changed from slightly relaxed to a more aggressive stance. Everyone saw the change and assumed this was some kind of a trap for this creature to get in close for the kill.

That's when they all heard what the alpha heard. Helicopters. Matoskah figured that these creatures probably didn't understand the helicopters were part of the effort to save the forest.

The alpha let out an angry growl, like when a dog first alerts to a threat. Matoskah had to act fast.

"Toothless, toss me your lighter."

Even though Toothless had just recently come to, he managed a fairly well-aimed toss to Matoskah.

Matoskah whistled to get the alpha's attention. He then pointed up at the sky in the direction of the incoming helicopters, making a motion like the rotors. Then, he lit Toothless' lighter, and took his water canteen off his belt. When he lit the lighter, the alpha took a step back, but Matoskah put it out to show it was okay. He re-lit the lighter, then raised his canteen above his head, and moved it towards the lighter's flame. Once he had it where he wanted it, he poured the water from the canteen on the lighter, dousing the flame. He then pointed back up to the sky and then back to his canteen. The alpha's body language seemed less aggressive, but it still stared into the sky, watching these mechanical birds come closer.

20

BATH TIME

"Air One to forward fire base. Come in, Mills."

The approaching pilots had no way of knowing what had transpired over the last hour.

"Air One to forward fire base. Over." Lieutenant Commander Martin "Al" Peak was on his drop run and wanted to make sure the ground crews were prepared.

Mills was in a cover position close to the cab of the downhill-facing truck, so she would be able to grab the mic and coordinate with the helicopter crews. Even though they were in a fight for their lives, they still had a job to do.

"Forward fire base to Air One. Good to finally hear your birds coming in. We're a mess down here. Something's been attacking us, and we're under cover. We can't expose ourselves, and the fire's moving up. So, drop away."

"Ten-four, Mills. I see your strobes. I don't see anything down there yet. Will do a quick look around after our drop. Who the hell attacks firefighters?"

Mills didn't want to mention anything about monsters over the airway. Her transmission could be heard by a lot of people, and she was sure they would think she was crazy.

"I'm with you there, Al. Probably some crazies, or something."

The alpha watched as the metal birds flew overhead. Something large hung from the bottoms of the birds. The sight was confusing to him. He was thinking of the trespasser's fire and the water he had poured on the flame. He didn't quite understand what he saw, but he watched these birds with great interest.

Peak brought the first water drop and lowered his altitude to a little over a thousand feet and hovered over the leading edge of the fire. When the bladder had stabilized, he released his payload of 2,500 gallons of water. The rotor wash whipped the water as it fell, and the crews below got a welcome dose of cold water sprayed on their location. Although most of the water made it to the fire, there was always some drift. Lieutenant Wilson came in right after Peak cleared the area, and another load was delivered. Instantly, steam from the water vaporizing obscured the leading edge for a moment. Lieutenant Commander Peak made as low a circle as he could with a water bladder hanging below his aircraft. The steam acted like a smoke screen, and he couldn't see any attackers on the ground.

"Sorry, Nance. I don't see anything within a couple hundred yards of your position. Heading back to the river for another load. Sun's gonna be up in a bit. Should help us find who's out there. See ya' in about forty-five."

Mills couldn't help but feel some relief. No attackers within 200 yards. She took a minute to enjoy the cooling of her face from the water drop. Everyone seemed reborn, looking skyward with their faces dripping from the cooling mist. Maybe their luck was about to change.

The betas that had attacked the command center were staying in the woodland shadows about 300 yards away, close enough to see their movements, but not so close as to be seen themselves. They, too, had watched the water rain from the metal birds. They did not understand it, but the cool mist felt good. They were ready to attack the trespassers again, but the betas would not move until the alpha signaled. And so, they waited.

The alpha watched the rain fall from the metal birds and understood the visual the trespasser had shown him. Water from the sky without a storm? What power did these trespassers have that they could make water fall from birds? Even though the tribe members would be considered highly intelligent, their reasoning abilities were limited. What they were seeing was definitely outside their abilities. All that would register was that rain from the metal birds was a good thing, and, somehow, these trespassers controlled them. The alpha was confused about what he was seeing, and his thoughts went to the trespassers in the caverns. Were they part of the same tribe as these? He needed to be sure. One thing he did understand — these trespassers and the ones below were trying to save his tribe's lands, and they would be protected.

Stumpy needed to clue Mills in on what was happening before anyone got hurt.

"Hey, Nance, Stumpy here. I need you to come up to our location asap."

Mills wasn't enthusiastic about leaving the relative safety of the trucks. Traveling to Stumpy's team meant she would be exposed to attack for several hundred yards. Not what she would call a prudent move.

"I'm not moving anywhere until I know those things are gone. They could be anywhere."

I understand what you're sayin', Nance. You're gonna have to trust me on this one. Oh, and one more thing. Leave the shotgun behind."

Mills was completely confused now. What the hell was Stumpy thinking? "Are you crazy, Sam? I'm not leaving the shotgun. It's a long damn way to your position, and I just might need to, I don't know, protect my damn self."

"I'm serious, Nance. Believe me. You will *not* be needing it."

Mills knew Stumpy wouldn't put her in any danger. But how could he possibly know she would be safe? What the hell was so important that she would need to leave the command trucks? One thing was for sure — she wasn't going to get any answers by staying put.

"Hey, Meyer, take the shotgun. I'm headin' up to Stumpy. Keep your heads down and be ready for the next bucket drop. Should be coming sometime in the next half hour or so."

"You sure, Nance? It's a long way up there, and we don't know where these things are."

"I know what you're sayin', but Stumpy wouldn't let me up there if it would put me in danger. Not sure what's up, but the answer is up there. I'll be back as soon as I can."

With that, Mills headed up to the forward position.

The alpha needed to signal to the others that the fight was over, for now. It let out three high-pitched whistles. This would let the betas below know not to attack. The senior beta answered with one whistle. That was all it took to stop all hostilities towards the trespassers. The betas didn't understand, but the alpha was their leader, and his will was law.

The alpha had let loose with the whistles without any warning to the crew, and it startled them. Mills was even more reserved about her relocating after she heard the whistles from above her and then the one close by below her. She felt alone and surrounded.

"What the hell was that all about, Jack?"

"I don't have a damn clue, Stumpy. Let's just see what happens. I don't think it's a bad thing, but I'm not sure."

The alpha watched these trespassers closely. Even though he felt they were helping, he wasn't completely trusting. His experiences with this tribe of beings in the past were mostly bad ones. He would watch a little longer.

As Mills made her way up the firebreak to Stumpy's position, the sun was breaking over the ridge above her, and she could barely make out the silhouettes of some of the crew. Even though the sun partially obscured her vision, it didn't look as though they were trying to stay under cover. The rising sun also kept her from seeing the alpha standing just off to the side of the crew. That changed as soon as she reached Stumpy and the crew. She froze when she saw it. Her blood felt turned to ice, and she couldn't muster any semblance of a word. She was only able to move again when Stumpy spoke to her.

"It's okay, Nance. Matoskah thinks he knows what this is and why we've been attacked."

"Holy shit, Sam. Are you sure? This thing's killed a bunch of people, including some of our friends. How can we be so sure we're not next?"

"Well... so far, so good. I needed you to see for yourself. I didn't want to put it out over the radio for a bunch of reasons. Who knows who's listening in on our radio transmissions."

Stumpy understood the importance of what the presence of this creature meant. He also knew that if they were to confirm the existence of, for lack of a better name, Bigfoot, even though these creatures were responsible for so many deaths, it wouldn't be right to put their existence out there. These creatures had an intelligence to them, and if they were to be discovered, there would be no end to the parade of people who wanted to bag one for their wall. Once word got out of the exact location of where a verified, active group of these were, there would be hundreds, if not thousands, of people flooding this mountain to get a picture or find some other evidence of the beast. The creatures would surely look at this as an invasion and would defend their lands, just as they had been doing over the last few days, and this would only end badly for both humans and these creatures. They could not let that happen.

"Nance, we need to keep these things under wraps. We can't let this out. No radio broadcasts. No pics. Nothing."

It took quite a bit of coaxing to convince Mills of this, but she eventually saw the truth in it. They would have to control the situation.

"Okay, I get it, Sam. But what about all the shit that's already gone out over the radio? I mean, we've said over and over that we were under attack by some*thing*, not some*one*. And we still don't know what the situation is with Captain Roberts and the others."

"I know you're worried about them, Nance, but I'm sure they're okay. They made it to cover before the fire, and it hasn't been that long since we last had contact. I'm sure we'll hear from them anytime, now. In the meantime, I've got an idea about how we can deal with this. The fire may just have provided us a way to handle this whole attacker thing."

Stumpy went on to explain that while he was working his original strike team's location, they had come across a large grizzly bear that had been killed when fire had super-heated a large Western Larch tree. These trees are heavy with resin. When the resin inside started to boil, the tree exploded. This is quite a common occurrence in forest fires, and it's one of the hazards the fire crews have to watch out for. Splinters from this explosion pierced the bear and killed it. If they got their stories straight, they could use the bear as their cover story. After all, it was well-known that grizzlies have a bit of a temper. Plus, the fire would burn any evidence of the contrary.

The alpha had been relatively still up to this point, watching the trespassers closely. He felt an uneasy stillness among the trespassers and sensed their fear. He was unsure of his next move. The one he had been communicating with and the one who had had the thunder stick seemed to lose their fear, which told the alpha now was the time. He needed to know about the others, the ones in his home. If they were part of this tribe, these ones would know. The alpha took one step towards Matoskah and grunted. This wasn't an angry grunt. It was softer, almost as if clearing its throat. Then it turned, as if to leave, but then stopped and looked back at Matoskah and grunted again. It was hard to explain, but everyone there seemed to understand.

"I think it wants me to follow it." Matoskah looked at Mills and Stumpy and, without hesitation, started to follow the alpha.

"Hang on, Jack. I'm going with you. Nance, get back down to the command trucks and explain to the guys what's going on, and then get those trucks up to the fire service road. We'll meet you up there as soon as we can."

"You sure about this, Sam?"

"Nope. Just seems to be the right thing to do. Besides, someone's got to inform the pilots doing the bucket dumps what we're doing. You can coordinate fire operations from the ridge line."

Mills was more than a little concerned about the situation. What did this creature have in store for her friends? After all, it and others had already killed several people. And how the hell was she going to explain to her crew back at the trucks what she had seen and the plan her and Stumpy came up with? She would need proof. She pulled out her cell phone and took a hasty pic of Stumpy, Jack, and the creature. It was of their backs as they headed out, but it would have to do. She would have a little time to figure out exactly how to explain things while she made her way back down to the command trucks. One thing kept rolling through her head. "No one's going to believe this."

"What the fuck did I just see? What's goin' on here, fellas?" Even though Toothless was still groggy, he had become conscious enough to see what was happening around him and was confused.

"Where the hell are Stumpy and Jack going? What the hell was that thing with them? Someone tell me *something!*"

While the crew calmed Toothless down and filled him in, Matoskah and Stumpy wondered where they were headed. Keeping up with this creature was difficult. This thing was huge but pushed through the thick brush and dense growth like a hot knife through butter. Not to mention its stride was at least three times longer than theirs. All the while, Stumpy and Matoskah seemed to snag on every branch and bramble. Several times, the alpha had to stop and wait for them to catch up. The farther they went, the steeper and rougher the terrain became, yet this creature never slowed down, never stumbled or made a misstep. It also made very little noise. In fact, the only discernible sounds were from the two humans. It seemed every step came with a twig snap, branch break, or a stumble. As experienced forest fire fighters, they were considered experts in managing terrain, but they were like toddlers in the woods compared to this creature. This thing wasn't even breathing hard.

They could hear the efforts to combat the fire from the helicopters but were out of the fight for now. The smoke from the fire and suppression efforts obscured their view of their way forward. At times, they weren't even able to see their large, hairy guide. Then, as if by design, the smoke cleared just enough for the two to see their destination. There, just a few feet in front of them, stood the alpha. He appeared to be stopped against the base of a rocky outcrop. Then, the alpha took a step to the right and was gone.

"Holy shit! Where'd it go?"

The two ran to where they had last seen the beast and, there, hidden behind an optical illusion of a solid rock wall was large a hole. It was completely hidden from view from all sides by a large boulder that matched the background rock. They could feel a cool breeze flowing out of the hole, and it smelled bad. It smelled like their hairy friend but times twenty. The smell was so strong, it almost knocked them back on their heels.

"Geez, that's bad, Jack. Smells like rot on a stick."

"You got that right. I'm masking up."

Matoskah pulled the bandanna from around his neck and affixed it like an Old West bandit.

"Hey, it may not eliminate the smell completely, but anything's better than full force."

Stumpy did the same thing, and the two disappeared into the dark hole.

21

EVER UPWARD

Mills started to put her and Stumpy's plan into action as soon as she returned to the command trucks. She would have to move quickly to mobilize the crew and get the trucks moving up the escape route to reach the fire service road above them before the fire overtook their position.

"All right, boys, let's get these trucks up the hill. Yancey, you take SP and get him in the lead truck. Take Jeffries with you. I'll follow with Pitts and Meyers in the other truck. We'll take Davidson's body with us. But first, I need to fill you all in on a couple things."

Mills explained everything to the disbelief of the crew. It was hard to convince them, until she showed them the picture she took.

"See that thing there? That's it. That's what's been attacking us. But, for now at least, it seems to have stopped. Matoskah thinks it's a being his tribe is familiar with. I don't know about that, but what I do know is this. We absolutely cannot tell anyone about this. I'm deleting this picture, and as far as I'm concerned, we were attacked by a wounded grizzly. I'm counting on *all* of you to back me up on this. It's important. I'll fill you in on more when we get to the top of the ridge. Now, help me get Davidson's body covered up and in the truck."

The crew was stunned by what they had just been told by their leader, a person they'd known to be level-headed and not prone to exaggeration or hysteria, a person they trusted with their lives. It didn't make sense. After all, people had died because of this thing. How could they just turn their backs on that? Then again, who would believe them? Hell, they barely believed it, and they were right in the middle of it. Maybe Mills was right. Maybe what else she had to say would help them understand things more clearly. For now, they had work to do.

"We're all loaded and ready, Nance. You good to go?" Mills could see Yancey was anxious to get moving.

"We're right behind you, Yance. It's a bit rough going up that trail, so take it slow, okay?"

"Slow it is, Nance."

"Forward command to Air One. Over."

"This is Air One. Go ahead, forward command."

"We're moving to the ridge. We'll contact you when we are secure. Over."

"Ten-four, Mills. See you at the top."

The heli-tack crews had delivered a total of six bucket drops between the two helicopters, and it had slowed the forward progress of the fire quite a bit. But even with almost 5,000 gallons of water unloaded with each drop, it would take days to get this fire under control. More air resources might need to be called in, but that was up to the fire crew leader. And, until it was determined he was dead or otherwise out of commission, that leader was Captain Robertson.

It took about twenty minutes for the trucks to reach the trail-blazing crew. They got them loaded in the two remaining trucks and placed Matthews' body in the second truck next to Davidson. Once everyone was secure, they continued to the ridge. In the few minutes it took to reach the top, no one said a word. Everyone was trying to come to grips with the loss of their crewmates and what they had actually faced. Mills was especially withdrawn as she pondered the fate of Captain Robertson and the others with him in the cave. Specifically, Ben Proctor. Her heart sank at the thought of the possibility losing him. She made a promise to herself that if Ben survived, she would never let things go unsaid between them. And what of Matoskah and Stumpy? All these thoughts were swimming in her head, and, on top of everything else, she had to find a way to protect the very thing that had brought them all this pain. It was time to gather the men and get their stories straight.

"All right, guys. Let's pull it in and get our heads on straight."

22

RESCUE

Stumpy and Matoskah put on their headlamps and entered the darkness of the cave. It was total darkness, yet the creature never seemed to need to adjust to the darkness. It just kept moving in deeper. At one point, it stopped and made three whistle noises and paused. When the creature stopped, so did Jack and Stumpy. They wondered what the whistles meant. It didn't take long to find out. After just a few seconds, two whistles echoed from deep within the cavern. There were more of them in there with them. That made the two men nervous. The alpha could sense their uneasiness and turned to face them. He gave a soft grunt and moved deeper into the darkness.

"Well, we've come this far. No turning back now." Stumpy almost sounded as if he was trying to convince himself to continue.

"I'm with, ya', Stumpy. Let's go."

"What the hell was that?" Adam Wallace was reacting to the whistling sounds they had all just heard. Three had come from a distance, but two seemed right there in the same space they were in.

"Calm down, Wallace. Probably just a bat or something." Captain Robertson knew it wasn't a bat or a bird. He'd never heard anything quite like that before. He leaned over to Proctor and whispered so only he could hear, "Get ready, Squatch. Somethin's comin'."

Proctor's muscles tensed as he strained to make anything out in the darkness. He thought he saw movement in the shadows — or was it just his mind playing tricks on him? Adrenaline flowed through his body as he worked hard to maintain his composure. After all, everyone who had come in contact with whatever they were dealing with had died. The odds were not in their favor.

As he and the others searched the shadows for anything that looked like their attacker, Proctor thought he saw a light.

"Hey, Cap, you see that? Is that a light up there?"

Captain Robertson focused on where Squatch was pointing, and he, too, thought he saw a light.

"Well, fellas, as far as I know, these things don't have flashlights."

Robertson decided to take a chance.

"Hello, up there! Captain Robertson here. Who's there?"

"Sh.... Stumpy thought he heard the faint sound of voices. The alpha had stopped and appeared to be allowing the two to go on by themselves.

"I thought I heard something too. Hard to tell."

The two men stood there, silent, listening for any other sounds. The alpha stepped back and gave that same soft grunt it seemed to make when it wanted the two men to do something.

"Well, let's keep going. We'll take it nice and slow."

They hadn't gone more than a few yards when they heard it again. It was faint and echoey but definitely a voice.

"Sounds like the captain. Hello, down there!"

Everyone heard Stumpy's voice respond to Captain Robertson's hail, and they let out a collective cheer.

"It's Stumpy!" Squatch couldn't believe it. It had to be Stumpy coming to his rescue. Not again; he didn't think he could handle another rescue by the chunky one.

"I'm never gonna live this down."

"Try the radio, Jack. See if we can pick up the captain on it in here."

"You hear me, Cap? Matoskah here. Come in."

The radios hadn't made any noise since the crew entered the caverns, but now, there was a fuzzy voice coming out of the walkies.

"Got you, Jack. Be careful. We're not alone in the cavern."

"Ten-four, Cap. We know. It's okay. We're coming to ya', so don't shoot."

"Ten-four, Jack. Watch your back."

Even though the cavern system had multiple open areas, they all connected back to the same main tunnel. There was lots of evidence that a large number of *something* was using this cavern system as shelter. The open areas were a mix of what appeared to be bedding areas. These areas had branches and pine boughs covering the floor that made up bedding, and other areas were covered in assorted animal bones. Obviously, this was where they ate. No wonder it was impossible to get proof of these creature's existence. They didn't stay above ground for long. Most animals ate at the kill site. These creatures brought their food inside where they could eat out of sight. The main passage eventually led Matoskah and Stumpy to the area where Robertson and the others had taken shelter.

"Cap, you down there?"

Robertson and the others were still on high alert, waiting for a possible attack from whatever they were sharing this cavern with, so when Stumpy's voice rang out just above them, they were all extremely relieved, and surprised.

"Down here, Sam!"

At the sight of Matoskah and Stumpy, Robertson and the others got up and headed to the two, all the while keeping their guard up against an attack.

"How'd you find us? How the hell did you know we were in here? And what the hell is on your hard hats? Is that a *face*?"

"Well, you're going to find this hard to believe, but here goes..."

While Stumpy was explaining what had unfolded to lead the two to their location, he could tell they were having a hard time buying it.

"Hey, Jack, maybe you'd better explain the new team logo. I think they need to hear it from the guy who figured it out."

Just out of sight from the trespassers below, the alpha watched as the ones he brought into his home met the others. They were together. Even though he felt they were helping the tribe, he didn't like them being in his lair. They needed to go. He would let them know it was time. He let out a short but aggressive whoop.

"Holy shit, Jack! I thought you said it understood we were on its side." Robertson was about to go back into full battle mode, when Matoskah stopped him.

"Hold on a second, Cap. Remember, if it wanted us dead, we would already be dead. This is where they live, and we are trespassing. I think it's just time to go."

"Well, you're leading the way. But I'm not letting our guard down. Not for one minute."

"Do me a favor, Cap. Don't point the shotguns at anything. They may take that as a threat, and we don't need that."

"I hope you're right, Jack. Our lives depend on it. Since you seem to have some kind of understanding about these things, you lead us out."

"No problem, Cap."

As the seven crew members made their way up the boulder field toward the main passage, Stumpy turned around to look at Proctor.

"Hey, Squatch, I was just thinking...saved your ass again, huh?" With that, Stumpy let out an evil little giggle.

"Yeah, yeah, yeah. Rub it in, stump boy. We ain't out of here yet."

About halfway up the boulder field, they all saw what had been guarding them from their hidden positions. There were three of them. They were obviously females; they had breasts. Hairy breasts, but breasts. They stood between six and six and a half feet tall and probably weighed close to 250 pounds or more. Robertson and the crew with him stopped when they saw them, but Matoskah and Stumpy just kept walking.

"It's okay, guys. They're letting us pass. You ain't seen nothin' yet."

Stumpy and Matoskah had smirks on their faces, knowing they were about to see the big one.

"Remember, no shootin', fellas. It's all going to be okay." Seeing that neither Stumpy nor Matoskah were carrying any weapons made the others trust that they would be safe. Still, it was unnerving.

When they reached the top of the boulder field and turned into the main passage, they could all see him. The alpha. He stood dead center of the passage as if asserting his authority one more time.

He had to let these trespassers know that it was only because he allowed them to live that they were alive. He would let them pass, but only after he was sure his power had been acknowledged. His facial expression changed to one of complete anger, but his body language didn't indicate he would attack. It was posturing, a common form of asserting power over subordinates in the great ape family. Even though these trespassers were not of the same tribe, they seemed to understand. To a man, they all sensed the power of the alpha and also felt they would live through this. But it didn't make it any more enjoyable.

Matoskah turned to the others. "Don't make eye contact. He'll view that as a threat to his authority, and judgement will be swift. Just look down and walk by as I do."

With those words, Matoskah lowered his head, opened his palms, and slowly walked past the alpha. The alpha let out a short, terse, huff as Matoskah passed. One by one, the others passed by in the same manner until they were all on the other side of the alpha. With one last aggressive grunt, the alpha turned and went back from where he had just been. He would check on his female tribe members and release the outside guard blocking where the crew had entered. The tribe's safety was his priority now. They had to be brought into the safety of the caverns to wait out the fire. What happened to these trespassers was no longer their concern.

Robertson and the crew made their way through the passage as it twisted upward towards the hidden opening just a few hundred yards away. The choking fire smoke would almost be relief from the overwhelming stench of the caverns. All along the way, they tried to make radio contact with the crew on the ridge, but the signal would not penetrate the cavern walls. The radios barely worked inside, even when just a few yards apart.

"This is gonna be one hell of a story to tell my children."

"Just make sure it's a goodnight story, Pederson. That'll make for some sweet dreams, for sure." Dutchauser and Pederson broke the tension that they were all feeling. Were they really going to be okay? Seemed like in every monster movie, everyone dies a horrible death just when they're about to make it out alive.

"You smell that, guys? It's smoke. We're gettin' close," Stumpy announced, and the crew's pace picked up almost to a trot. Soon, they would be free of the caverns and be facing an enemy they were more familiar with: fire.

"There it is, fellas. Freedom!" Stumpy was the first to stumble out into the smokey outside world. One by one, they exited the caverns, and, although the smoke was thick, they all took deep breaths to rid their noses of the putrid aroma that permeated the caverns.

"Get Mills on the radio. Let her know we're safe and coming to her."

"Roger that, Cap. Strike team one to forward command. This is Stumpy. Come in, Nance."

"Forward command. Good to hear your voice. You guys okay?"

Roger that, Nance. We're headin' your way. Even bringin' a few more with us. We got what's left of Cap's crew. They're a little beat up but good."

"That's great news, Sam. We are set up on the ridge. Heli-tack crews are pounding the fire with bucket drops. Looks like they've really slowed the fire. We might even get some rest before we regroup."

"Sweet! See you, soon. Out."

Her thoughts immediately went to Ben Proctor. What's *left* of Cap's crew? Who's missing? What if it's Ben?" A numbness came over her, and she felt sick to her stomach.

She was brought back to reality with the sound of the heli-tack pilots checking in.

"Air One to forward fire command. Come in, Mills. Air One checking in. Over."

"Forward fire command to Air One. We are set. Over."

"Good deal, Nance. We're making our final run before refueling. We'll be out of the fire zone for about ninety minutes. Looks like we knocked it back a bit. You should be able to establish a new anchor point from your new position. Hey, any more on the attacks on your crew? We haven't seen anything from the air."

And so it began. The start of their cover story. She had to sound convincing, or the story wouldn't fly.

"Ten-four on your refuel, Al. And, yeah, we figured out what was responsible for the attacks. Seems like we had a wounded grizzly causing all the ruckus. Between the fire and some pretty strange coincidences, we got our brains all in a twist and thought some crazy person was after us. Looks like the bear's done. Pitts says he saw a grizzly all covered in blood fall into the tree line below us. Pretty sure the fire overtook it by now."

"A grizzly? They can be real ornery when hurt, but wow. That's crazy. They're not normally this far south, but there was one caught and collared even farther south, near Athol, just last fall. Guess they're expanding their territory. That's good news, right? See you soon. Air One out."

"Ten-four. Out."

"I think he bought it. Now, let's make sure we *all* stick to the bear story."

Mills looked over at the rookie, Brian Pitts.

"Remember, Pitts. You saw the bear running away, right?"

"Yes, ma'am. I got it. No problem."

There wasn't much time for resting. Mills needed to set up a new anchor point to fight the fire. An anchor point is where the crews start to form a fire line, and a new one was needed to keep the fire from cresting the ridge. She would need both Stumpy's and Captain Robertson's strike teams if they were to have a chance at containing this fire. Once the fire was contained, it would feed into itself and self-extinguish. At least, in theory. The good news was that the winds had died down considerably, they had air support now, and the ridge was more rocks than trees. They had a chance. If the fire got past them here, it was pretty much a straight shot through heavy forest and several hundred homes and farms to reach the town of Spirit Lake. It would be a nightmare of evacuations down gravel roads and two main paved roads, Spirit Lake Cutoff Road and Highway 41. Both routes ran north-south more or less and were only two lanes. The County Sheriffs and the Idaho State Police would have to go door to door to evacuate people. Mills hoped that would not be necessary, but residents would need to be put on alert.

There are three levels of wildfire evacuation alerts. Level one is the lowest concern and means residents should be prepared to evacuate. Level two means evacuation is likely, and level three is for when evacuation is mandatory. The residents were currently under a level-one evacuation alert. It was up to the commander of the resources on the fire line to make recommendations for upgrading the alerts. Mills would defer to Captain Robertson when he arrived at their new position. After all, with both Stumpy and Robertson back in action, she was third in seniority. In her mind, though, she played out what she would do if asked to provide a recommendation. She was confident a level two should be enacted. This would allow the residents in the potential path of the fire to at least get their animals trailered and bags in their vehicles. Most residents of this rugged territory already had bug-out bags ready to go.

It wouldn't be too long before the remnants of teams A and B made it to the ridge, forty-five minutes or so. Mills would let her crew get some food in their bellies and hydrate before setting the fire line.

"Okay, guys, let's take thirty to catch our breath. Get some chow and get plenty of water in you. Gonna be a long, hot day."

Robertson, Stumpy, and their rag-tag crew made their way through the dense pine thickets. The terrain was steep, and the heavy growth of young trees made it difficult to make great time. But they were only about a quarter of a mile from the ridge and Mills' crew. They were beat up, and their supplies were low. Most of the water and food was on the truck they had to leave behind. And that truck had long since been destroyed by the fire. They had no idea they were down to just two banged-up trucks. Stumpy hadn't told the captain about the loss of Davidson and Matthews, or the injury to Frye (Spud).

It was time to fill him in.

"Hey, Cap, you need to know we've lost some men on this fire. Davidson and Matthews are gone, and Spud's hurt pretty bad. It's only because of Jack that we're still alive. If it weren't for the fact he's Kalispel and his grandfather's stories about this lost tribe, we'd all be dead. I'm sure those things we passed in the caverns weren't there by accident. I think after they did us in, you were next. I think it's best if you let Jack fill you in. It's a hell of a story, and the funny thing is, it's all true. See this logo on my hard hat? That's the mark of the creatures. They put that all over these woods. Hard to see 'em, 'cause they're hidden pretty good. Jack found them, though. Thank God he did, or we wouldn't be havin' this little talk. Just lettin' you know, 'cause you're gonna see this mark a lot."

Robertson was quiet for a few minutes as he took stock of their losses and what Stumpy was telling him. It was difficult to swallow. Then he remembered the greeting they got from Jimmy Two Horns and the tribal elders when they first arrived. There might just be something to this Native stuff.

"Hey, Jack, fill me in on what you know about these things. It'll take our minds off the hump up this ridge."

So Matoskah started from the beginning, covering everything he could remember from his grandfather's stories and tribal legends. He shared his thoughts on why they had been attacked and how, with a little luck, they were able to come to some kind of understanding with these beings. Matoskah also explained why they needed to keep the existence of them a secret. It was good that the other crew members with Robertson in the caverns were able to hear this story too. With everything that had happened to them, they were more inclined to avenge their friends than to save these things. But after Matoskah's story, they seemed to understand, but that didn't mean they were happy about it. One thing's for sure, though. None of them would ever look at the forest the same again. As forest fire fighters, they had an innate respect for nature and the fine balance that kept it working. But now, they would always wonder if they were being watched and being judged.

The trek to the ridge was difficult. Most of the way was covered in dense pine groves and dead-falls. And with the smoke, they could only see a few feet in front of them. All they knew was the ridge was up, so up they went. Having Matoskah tell his story broke the claustrophobic and strenuous journey. About the time he had finished telling all he knew, they broke out of the thick growth and onto a solid granite rock bulge that gently sloped downward towards the old fire service road. They didn't see any sign of the new command position, but it couldn't be far.

"They gotta be north of us. When we started from the top of the trail, we cut and headed south to the caverns. Shouldn't take long."

Stumpy had taken a GPS waypoint when he and Matoskah left the crew. "Let's see if you're right, Jack."

Sure, enough, Matoskah was correct. According to the GPS, the waypoint Stumpy recorded was to the north and 200 yards below them.

"When will you pale-faces learn? We Native Americans are part compass, you know."

With the tensions of imminent attacks from giant, hairy monsters all but gone, the fire crew was starting to relax and get back to the more normal life-and-death stress of the dangers of fighting forest fires.

As the adrenaline burned off, the crew felt worn down. Their feet felt like anvils attached to their legs, and brain fog was setting in. They made their way down the smooth granite boulder by sitting and sliding down to the overgrown fire service road. By the time they started towards the new command post, they could hear the helicopters bringing the next round of bucket drops in from the river, and that refocused the men.

Captain Robertson looked up, smiled, and turned to the others behind him. "Ah... the sound of angels from heaven, boys. Maybe we'll get this damn fire under control soon, and we can get the hell off this mountain."

There was a collective, "Hell, yeah" from the crew, and they picked up their pace.

"Fire base command to forward fire command Hoodoo. Come in, Mills."

The radio had been fairly quiet the last few hours, and the call from the command center surprised Nancy.

"Forward fire command. Go ahead."

"Good news, Nance. We've got some relief heading your way. Two crews from St. Marie's are en route and should be there by noon. What is your current location?"

"That is great news, command. We are anchored at 48.078 degrees north and 116.95 degrees west on old fire service road 147. It's a bit overgrown but seems passable."

"Ten-four, Nance. Will pass info along. How's it going up there?"

"We're pretty beat up, but we're hanging in there. We lost two more guys. Turns out we had a rogue grizzly up here. But the fire took care of him. Good news is we found Captain Robertson and his crew. They lost a man to a fall, but the rest of them seem okay. They should rejoin us pretty soon."

The smoke had changed from the thick, acrid, ash-laden cloud to blue-white smoke, thanks to the bucket drops. The water cut down on the ash in the smoke, and there was more water vapor, or steam. This was good news. It meant the fire was slowing down; its forward progress was being affected by all the water raining down.

"Hey, Stumpy, let's let Mills know we are on the old fire road and heading her way."

"Roger, Cap. Strike Team A to forward fire command. Come back, Mills."

Mills had been waiting anxiously for this call. Even though it had only been about forty-five minutes, it seemed like hours since the last position call to Nancy. She had been quietly praying for Ben Proctor to be safe, for his return from the ordeal he and his team had endured. There was no denying how she felt about him anymore, and she had already told herself she would let him know. If only she got the chance. She took a deep breath and tried to sound professional.

"Good deal. We are set up right on the road, so you won't miss us. Fire case command just let us know we're getting help from St. Marie's. Should be here midday."

"That's great news, Mills. Maybe we'll get a handle on this thing after all."

With the extra crews coming in, Captain Robertson felt they may actually contain this fire before it could regain momentum. But it would take more than the extra crews and some bucket drops. They would need serious aerial support. They would need several drops of Phos-Chek, the red chemical fire retardant. The high winds the crews had dealt with at the beginning of this fire wouldn't have allowed for these drops, but the wind was dying down now. Robertson would evaluate this tactic when they rendezvoused with Mills' strike team. She had a better handle on where they were with the fire since his team had been stuck in the caverns and out of communication with outside resources. He would rely on her knowledge of the fire to help make that call. It wasn't far now. Robertson and the others could hear voices coming from somewhere in the smoke.

Mills moved to the southern edge of the command location so she would be the first to see the guys coming in. She had hoped it didn't look too obvious to the rest of her crew, but at the same time, she really didn't care what anybody thought. After all, worrying what others would think is why she hadn't told Ben how she felt. The events of the past couple of days had shown her how quickly life could change, how suddenly someone could be taken, and without warning. She had decided she couldn't count on having another day or another opportunity that would be better or more convenient. There was only now, today, this moment. It did not matter what the others thought anymore. The funny thing was, everyone else already knew.

Body language is a hard thing to control; it comes from the subconscious. It's a subtle language that has been around since the dawn of man. People pick up and understand body language no matter the spoken language; even those who speak different languages speak the same language of the body. It's almost universal.

That said, the whole crew knew how Mills felt about Proctor and how Proctor felt about Mills. They all felt it was a good match.

She tried to look nonchalant as she strained to see through the smoke. She could hear the men walking on the hard scrabble of the road. Then, she started to make out the shadowy figures of the crew as they traversed the ridge. They reminded her of ghosts materializing out of mist. As each got closer, ghosts were exactly what they looked like, soot-covered and exhausted ghosts. Captain Robertson was the first to reach her.

"Welcome to forward fire command, Cap. Boy, am I glad to see you."

"Nancy, you have no idea how happy I am to be here. Thought I'd never see the light of day again."

"I hate to say it, but I thought *none* of us were ever going to see another day. Who'd have thought we would've been in such a situation? Nothing in the manual about encounters with Bigfoot."

The whole time Mills was talking with the captain, her eyes were fixed on the men as they reached the command post. After the captain came Matoskah and Wallace. Then Pederson. A few seconds later, Dutchauser. There was a bit of a gap, and Stumpy came out of the smoke.

"Hey, Nance, glad to see me? You should be because, well, I saved Squatch, *again*."

Stumpy turned and made a grand gesture with his arm as if to say, "Ta-da... Here he is." And with that, Ben Proctor emerged from the smoke.

Mills was overcome with emotion, and tears flowed without warning. All else faded from her sight, and all she could see was Ben with his stupid, goofy grin on his face. "Hey, Nance, I was think—"

Before he could finish his thought, Nancy made a dash for him, almost knocking the captain over, and jumped into his arm, smothering him with a huge bear hug.

Everyone around them cheered, and Captain Robertson even mumbled, "About damn time." The only one who seemed surprised was Proctor. His nickname should have been Clueless, not Sasquatch, but it was a pleasant surprise. Ben had been attracted to Mills almost from the day they met but had never let on, at least not knowingly. There it was, again. The unspoken language. Body language. All living creatures speak this language and all living creatures understand it, even across species. All one has to do is tune in to it. It's just that some are better at it than others. The term *a woman's intuition* comes to mind.

Suddenly, Mills felt exposed; her feelings were out there for all to see, and she loosened her hug and whispered into Proctor's ear, "When this is all over, we should go out."

Ben Proctor felt a little dizzy. His heart was racing, and he had that tingly feeling deep inside. He wanted to respond with something witty, something that would save his ego from being dinged. Instead, all he could muster was, "Sounds great." Sounds *great*? What kind of lame response was that? So much for witty. The rest of the crew got a laugh out of it.

"Geez, Squatch. You'd think a big, strong man like you could come up with something better than, 'Sounds great.' Stumpy loved taking jabs at Proctor, especially when he couldn't make a snappy comeback.

"Okay, okay. I hate to break up you lovebirds, but we *do* have a job to do, and fire don't wait for love." It was all Captain Robertson could do to keep from laughing at the ridiculous situation that had finally brought these two together. It took almost dying from a raging fire while facing off with a tribe of Bigfoot-type creatures hellbent on finishing off those the fire spared, and, to top off, actually coming to an agreement with the creatures so they could return to fighting the fire that might end up killing them anyway. What the hell was he going to put in his fire report? How could he possibly explain what really happened? He couldn't.

"So, Mills, explain to me exactly what you've told command about what's been happening. We need to be on the same page. All of us. That means we need to get Slim in the loop."

Shit! She had almost forgotten about Slim. He was airlifted at the very beginning, and they'd had no communication with him since.

They could only hope he hadn't seen anything that would contradict the narrative.

With that, Mills and Proctor slowly released their hug, however reluctantly. They looked into each other's eyes with that look of understanding of just where they were with their feelings. Then they switched into firefighting mode. Love would have to wait.

The fire crews re-established their fire line at the crest of the ridge. Captain Robertson would man the forward fire command to coordinate the water and Phos-Chek drops and direct the crews from St. Marie's when they arrived. He would keep Frye with him until they could medevac him out to treat his crushed fingers. They should be able to get him off the mountain when St. Marie's arrived.

23

AND SO IT GOES

And so it went. Over the next ten days, the Northern Idaho Panhandle crews of Bonner County and St. Marie's were able to fight back the fire and get total containment. The activities of the crews did not go unnoticed.

The alpha kept watch, taking in all he saw and trying to understand the strange nature of these humans. He would never grasp the technology or the ways that were used to put out the fire in its lands, but he did understand one thing: Without these trespassers, they may have lost all their homelands. His tribe would forever be more careful in how they responded to trespassers in their lands.

When the fire crews finally left the mountain, Jimmy Two Horns and his tribal elders were there to greet them. It was quite the spectacle. Dressed in full Native regalia and performing traditional victory dances, they looked spectacular. And for Jackson Matoskah, it had a deeper meaning. He felt a renewed sense of self and a connection with his tribal roots he had never known before. It would be different for him now. He would proudly carry the title of Kalispel and seek to be more active in tribal matters. As his truck passed the spectacle, he made eye contact with Jimmy Two Horns. Jimmy stopped his dance and gave a nod, as if to tell Jack, "Well done, young man, well done."

Matoskah could almost hear the words, as if they were actually spoken to him.

Nancy Mills and Ben Proctor had their date. Saying it went well would be the understatement of the year. Their love for each other would grow, and by the following fire season, they were engaged. Their wedding was set for late fall, after the fire season.

2015 marked one of the busiest fire seasons for North Idaho in quite some time. There were over 300 forest fires in Idaho that year. In fact, the fires had stretched fire resources so thin that there were many fires in remote or difficult terrain that fire crews weren't even sent to fight. The fires that were fought cost over $80 million in fire suppression.

The Bonner County crews suffered the highest casualties of the season, with four confirmed dead: George Ludlow, Austin Matthews, Lloyd Davidson, and a fourth, Jesse Moore, presumed dead, although his body was never found. Ludlow's body was recovered once the fires were put out. The bodies of Brandon and Steve Rucker, the two brothers who accidentally started the fire to begin with, were also never found. There were also two fire crew members injured, Paul "Slim" Garrett and Brian "Spud" Frye. Both would make full recoveries, although Slim would suffer occasional migraines from his head injury.

The incidents on Hoodoo Mountain were attributed to a wounded grizzly and unstable terrain, which caused rockslides that damaged the trucks. The fire had completely destroyed the trucks to the point of making any forensic study impractical. Although this was the official story, investigators Bob Van Buren and Lieutenant Randy Thomas never fully bought the official report. They had poured over recordings of the radio transmissions, and the wounded grizzly bear story only came up towards the end of the violence that took the lives of the Rucker brothers and the fire crew members. Up until then, it sounded like the crews were under attack from someone or something else. There wasn't a lot for them to go on, other than the depositions from each crew member, where each corroborated the grizzly bear story. Add to that, that there were no remains found of the Ruckers or fire crew member Jesse Moore; it just didn't add up.

It's very rare for a fire to completely erase all parts of a body. To cremate a human body requires 1,400 to 1,800 degrees. While the average forest fire burns at 1,472 degrees, it rarely completely consumes all the bones, and especially not all the bones of three humans from different areas of the fire. Possible? Yes. Probable? No. The body of the grizzly bear was found; however, a necropsy of the body did not find any evidence of human remains or DNA. Again, fire could have destroyed that evidence, but it was highly unlikely that *all* the evidence would have been eliminated. With no corroborating evidence, and no one on the fire crew willing or able to tell a different story, the detectives were left with only one choice. So they closed the case and listed the deaths as accidental.

It is said that time heals all wounds. That is especially true with Mother Nature. The burned and scarred areas of Hoodoo Mountain grew back. The young shoots attracted deer, elk, moose, and other animals back to the mountain. During the time it took for nature to run its course, the tribe survived by raiding the valley lands below their mountain. The animals that survived the fire simply moved where there was abundant food, and so did the tribe. They would follow the food but return to their caverns to feed and stay hidden. But making foraging trips to the lowlands could prove risky. There were many humans living along the base of the mountain, and most of them hunted the same food as the tribe. They would stick mostly to the night to hunt, but this was not always how things worked out, and every once in a while, someone would glimpse one of them. Fortunately, catching fleeting glimpses and hearing strange noises and even finding footprints didn't bring much attention to the tribe. Most stories of sightings were explained away as misidentified animals or imagination.

For the Bonner County fire crews, the tribe was more than just real; it had become their mascot, so to speak. Captain Robertson had team patches made up with the symbol of the tribe on it. Under the symbol, *Fire Devils* was embroidered. Each team member, new and old, would be issued one to be sewn onto their right sleeve. There were also heavy-duty stickers that bore the same symbol and words to be placed on the front or back of their hard hats. Even their new trucks got the logo painted on the doors. For those who survived the ordeal on Hoodoo Mountain, it was a badge of honor and a protective emblem never to be mocked or disrespected. For the new members, it simply meant they were one of the Devils, and the story of how their logo came about would not be told to them. It was simply a cool patch they got to wear.

Oh, there were stories and rumors about what really happened on Hoodoo Mountain in July of 2015. And, as with most stories like that, the tale got taller, the monsters got bigger, and the hero's were more heroic. But with that, the stories become more unbelievable, thereby inadvertently protecting the tribe even more.

But there were other stories that come from the mountain. Stories of people feeling watched. Stories of giant, hairy creatures moving in the shadows. Strange sounds that no one could identify that would be attributed to the Hoodoo Howler, a Bigfoot-type creature rumored to inhabit the mountain. There were even reports of people going missing up on the mountain, disappearing without a trace. People even found articles of clothing and other personal belongings all over the North Idaho ranges, scattered randomly in remote areas frequented by hunters and hikers. But, experts would say there was no way a large, bipedal animal could go undetected for so long. Most likely, people were mistaking a large bear for their sightings.

One thing's for sure, experts don't know everything; they only know what they *think* they know. There are others who know better. One could ask the Fire Devils, but they aren't saying anything.

EPILOGUE

"Where you goin'?" Jean Brewer was still wrapped up in the covers not wanting to get out of bed on this crisp October morning.

The first hint of frost was on the lawn, and the house was chilly. The Brewers heated their home solely with a wood stove, and Chuck wasn't ready to start the wood splitting routine just yet.

"I'm gonna check that game camera I put up over on that trail. It's been a couple weeks since I checked it."

"Okay, but when you get back, I want a fire." Chuck grunted and grumbled as he headed out the door, but he managed an "All right" before he closed it.

He had hung the camera on a game trail that ran between the property next door and theirs. The trail cut between the two properties from the main trail, which ran through a small valley below their properties. Chuck had hung the camera so it would only take pictures if the animal was at least six feet tall. The trail came up a fairly steep hill, so he hung the camera pointing out over the down slope. Unless the animal was six feet tall, the camera wouldn't pick it up. There weren't many six-foot animals in the area. Maybe a moose — a *big* moose.

When he got to the tree where he had hung the camera, he noticed it was missing. His first thought was that someone had found it and stolen it. But who would come over here? The property behind his was thirty acres of vacant land, the property next door was still for sale and vacant, and the main gate was closed and locked. It didn't make any sense. Besides, the camera had been hung with a chain that was locked with a padlock.

He looked closer at the tree and noticed a large gouge in the bark, like someone had ripped the chain off the tree. The only way to do that was to hook it up to a truck or something. So he went down to the valley to look for tire tracks or some other clue. That's when he saw it. The chain was hung up in a small tree, and the lock was broken. And there were no tire tracks.

"What the hell?" He kept looking around, hoping to find his camera. After all, game cameras were expensive. He walked around for about thirty minutes before he spotted his camera. It was smashed to pieces where it had hit a large rock. "Who the hell would do something like this? That's just being mean." He picked up the camera to see if the memory card was still in it. It was. He just kept thinking, *Who would do this and leave the memory card?* He hoped the card had a picture of the person that had destroyed his camera. Maybe he would recognize him and could get him to buy him a new camera.

"What took you so long? I'm freezing." Jean didn't like walking on cold floors, and no fire in the stove meant the floor was freezing.

"Sorry, babe, but some asshole busted up my camera. Took me a bit to find the damn thing. Whoever did it's an idiot. Look, they left the card in the camera. Probably got a good pic of the guy that did it."

"Well, before you get all into your detective work, light me a fire, please. It's cold in here."

"All right, all right. It *is* a bit nippy in here. Guess it's time to start loading the firewood onto the porch."

After the fire was burning hot, chuck headed to his computer to load the memory card. "Well, it shows we got twelve pics on here."

Chuck had set up the camera so that when it was triggered, it would take three pictures in sequence. With twelve pictures on the card, it meant whatever tripped the camera was moving fast. When he initially set the camera up, he had tested it with himself walking up the trail at a good pace. During the test, the camera took twenty-four pictures of Chuck before he reached it.

"Must've been runnin' up that damn trail."

The first two pictures had virtually nothing in them. Just a light, fuzzy, curved line at the bottom. The third picture looked like a head. A *human*-like, head. But no facial features — just what looked like a fuzzy, white, human-like head. "What the hell is that?" The next two pictures looked like a thick-necked head on shoulders — still just white fuzz, no details. The next picture was completely whited out. That meant whatever was in front of the camera was blocking the *whole* lens. The lens was over seven feet off the ground. The next picture looked as if whatever it was had been moving off to the side. Then two pictures of nothing. The next picture showed what looked like a hand reaching over the top of the camera. The next was all whited out again. The last picture was the strangest. It was all white with one exception, what looked like an eye. It wasn't a moose eye or a deer eye. It also wasn't a human eye. But the picture didn't have enough detail to determine what it was. "Jean! Take a look at this."

The two studied the pictures for almost an hour and came up with the same conclusion. It looked like Bigfoot. It took them a few days, but they decided to report what they found to a local Bigfoot-hunting group. After several hours of questions and investigating the camera and where it was found, the group determined that the Brewers had most likely been visited by a sasquatch or bigfoot and said to keep a sharp eye out for future encounters. They also suggested the creature had probably come to their property because of the recent fires. They surmised the fire had run it out of its normal territory, and it was probably hungry. It was also unlikely to return unless its habitat was threatened again. That gave Jean some comfort, as she had been unsettled since she first saw it running across the field next door. After all, not many people want Bigfoot as a neighbor. Whether or not the creature ever returned to the Brewers, Chuck knew they had a bigfoot, or something like that, as a neighbor. And neither he nor Jean would look at the woods or stories of Bigfoot sightings the same way again.

There is a Native American saying: *I hope there is an animal somewhere that has never been seen, and I hope no one ever sees it.*

ABOUT M.C. PEAK

I've been an avid outdoorsman most of my life. I spent many years hiking and camping in the Blue Ridge Mountains of Virginia before moving to North Idaho, where I continued to pursue my love of the outdoors. The wildlife was bigger and more dangerous, but also more majestic, and I thoroughly enjoyed the moose that overwintered on our property. The many Bigfoot sightings in that area, the ongoing Bigfoot research that went on, and the many Native American historical accounts of sightings, as well as some personal experiences, are what inspired me to write the book *Hoodoo*.

I have since retired and moved to the Upper Peninsula of Michigan to be closer to family, but I continue to enjoy the great outdoors in a town aptly named Paradise. I also continue to write. Who would have thought there would be a high Bigfoot presence here in the UP? My interest in the Native American understanding of nature and our place in it has inspired another book, about a little known cryptid in and around Lake Superior that will, hopefully, be coming out soon.

I hope you enjoyed reading *Hoodoo*. Thank you.

AFTERWORD

Go to hangaripublishing.com to learn more about the Authors and stay up to date with their newest releases.

www.ingramcontent.com/pod-product-compliance
Lightning Source LLC
Chambersburg PA
CBHW061738120626
46550CB00005B/1822